W9-BMZ-409

ENTERTAINING

Angels

ANNIE CHAPMAN
HEIDI CHAPMAN BEALL

HARVEST HOUSE PUBLISHERS

EUGENE, OREGON

ENTERTAINING ANGELS
Copyright © 2009 by Annie Chapman and Heidi Chapman Beall
Published by Harvest House Publishers
Eugene, Oregon 97402
www.harvesthousepublishers.com

Chapman, Annie.
   Entertaining angels / Annie Chapman and Heidi Chapman Beall.
      p. cm.
   Includes bibliographical references.
   ISBN 978-0-7369-2475-7 (pbk.)
   Hospitality—Religious aspects—Christianity. I. Beall, Heidi Chapman. II. Title.
   BV4647.H67C43 2009
   241'.671—dc22

                                                                    2008026026

Annie's Acknowledgments

Anyone who has ever tried to write a year-end Christmas letter knows the enormous amount of effort it can take. Putting a book like this together would be impossible without the help of many people.

To all the ladies who filled out surveys. Your insights, stories, and suggestions were valuable beyond description. You made this book so much better because of your contributions. Thank you!

To all the folks at Harvest House Publishers for being God's instruments in helping me communicate a message placed in my heart and soul by the Lord. Extra-special thanks to Barbara Gordon (what a terrific editor you are) and Terry Glaspey, who thought a hospitality book with a little different twist and emphasis was an idea worth pursuing. Thank you!

I want to thank my daughter, Heidi, for agreeing to jump in and get her literary feet wet...even though she was already doing the most incredible job on the face of the earth—raising a daughter and growing another human being. You were a helpful, inspirational, and fun coworker on this book. Thank you, little Josie, for waiting to be born until after the deadline. Thank you, Lily, for being my little "guest" and teaching me to pass the torch of God's love on to the next generation.

To all of you who have blessed me with your presence through the years. Some were invited for a visit while others were unidentified angels sent for a greater purpose. You have taught me to see hospitality as an opportunity to see Jesus more clearly.

And I saved the best for last. To my husband, Steve, the best editor, writer, creative visionary, and puzzle-put-togetherer in the whole world. You've taken the pieces of this book and connected them into a coherent message. I am always amazed at your carefully crafted ability and your God-given talent. You are outstanding, and I thank God each day for bringing you into my life. In my heart, the day I married you, March 29, 1975, is second only to my receiving Christ as my Lord and Savior. Please don't ever die... or at least let me die first.

Heidi's Acknowledgments

My love of hospitality started when I was just a wee little girl. I remember watching my mom prepare for company. So much thought and effort went into making guests feel welcomed and loved. One way she showed her passion for service was having dinner ready the moment her guests arrived. No one ever had to wait around or help peel potatoes. I also watched my mom scrub floors and clean bathrooms at her mother's house when her mother was too sick to do the work herself. That's where I learned the art of true hospitality. Mom, thank you for teaching me what showing God's love to others is all about…and also for including me in this book project. I am in no way worthy to write beside you, but what an honor to have my name next to yours!

Dad, thank you for helping me in my maiden writing voyage. Thank you for being patient and not making too much fun of my novice scribbles. I couldn't have done this without your help.

Tish Beall, thank you for the wonderful ways you've blessed me throughout the years. I've learned so much from watching you live out Scripture. You are an angel who spends mornings and nights taking care of your dear mother and making sure your family has everything they need. I can only strive to be that giving.

Thank you to my father-in-law, Emmitt Beall Sr., for giving us the idea to write this book. You didn't know what you started when you wrote "just push the button" on that coffeemaker! I couldn't ask for a better father-in-law.

Emmitt and Lily—thank you for being supportive through this busy time. Our lives are all about to change with the addition of another little Beall. Emmitt, you've been so patient and understanding. God has blessed me with a husband who believed I could cowrite this book and a daughter who, on at least one occasion, played quietly with her toys so I could work. Thank you!

Contents

THE HANDS OF LOVE

BY STEVE CHAPMAN

The travelers were weary from the long highway
They looked for rest at the end of the day
And at her door they heard the sweet sound
"Come on in and set yourself down."

She poured the cold water
And served the warm bread
With kind conversation
Then she turned down their bed
They whispered "thank You"
To God up above
For touching them gently
With His hands of love

She was up long before the sun in the east
And gathered the fare for their morning feast
And she sent them on traveling, rested and filled
With the wounds of the highway doctored and healed

But she didn't know—

When she poured the cold water
And served the warm bread
With kind conversation
When she turned down their bed
She did it for angels
From God up above
And He smiled when she touched them
With His hands of love
Her hands were His hands of love[1]

Apple Pie, Anyone?

Generations of women helped put this book together. I (Annie) have been blessed with wonderful role models who were well skilled when it came to reaching out to others with hands of love. One woman who especially contributed to the motivation to write this book has long since passed away. Grandmother Naomi Alice Halbrieb Eckard was born in the 1880s. She was a living illustration of the heart and soul of hospitality.

The amazing thing about Grandma Naomi was that she demonstrated her unforgettable hospitality without the benefit of the niceties we associate with entertaining. She never owned a beautiful tablecloth or had lovely centerpieces or fragrant candles to adorn her table. Her dishes were not fine china, and she didn't possess crystal or silver. She served numerous meals to an incalculable number of guests on an assortment of mismatched, often chipped, dime-store plates. Her stemware consisted of a variety of jelly glasses. She didn't have electricity, indoor plumbing, or central heat and air conditioning. She had none of the conveniences or finery many of us assume we must have to entertain guests. What she did possess was a sincere desire to be gracious to others. Out of her great poverty she taught the richness of hospitality.

My mother, Sylvia, the youngest of Grandma Naomi's six children, commented one day,

> I grew up thinking that my mom didn't like apple pie because

I always saw her giving her slice to others to eat. I didn't realize at the time that what gave her more pleasure than the sweetness of the pie was the smile on someone else's face. When someone would show up at our door, and they often did, my mother would take her plate of food and give it to her guests, often leaving nothing for her to eat.

Because we were so poor, my mom had to sell the few eggs our old chickens would lay. We desperately needed the few cents we could get for them. On more than one occasion I saw my mom take the single egg she held back to feed her family of eight and creatively provide for everyone. She would make a skillet of "poor man's flour gravy," crack the lone egg and put it into the grease, flour, and water concoction and joyfully say, "Now we all get some egg to eat!"

In addition to Grandma Naomi's example, my mother was equally hospitable. She also had six children and lived in a little four-room house with no indoor plumbing. With limited resources she opened our home wide and made everyone who came to her door feel wanted and appreciated.

I can't name the day and time when I felt the baton for showing hospitality slip into my hand, but I know it did. Hospitality is such a wonderful way to pour God's tender love into the lives of others. Although my daughter, Heidi, never met her Great-Grandmother Naomi and had too few years of knowing her Grandmother Sylvia, I'm grateful that I can see the hospitality gift of our ancestors each time she responds to the needs of those who come into her life.

When Heidi and I talk about the impressive way my mother and my grandmother showed hospitality with so little finery, we both agree that with all the tools we have, we not only have more opportunities, we also have an even greater responsibility to be God's hands of love.

The many discussions, planning sessions, and joys we've had walking the aisles of our local shops looking for entertainment tools led to cooking up this book. Heidi and I hope that in the following pages you'll discover the *how* of hospitality and also the *why* and *joy* of entertaining. There is nothing as sweet as seeing the smile on someone's face who has been the recipient of the fruit of your hospitality...the best "apple pie" ever!

1

Opening Our Hearts and Homes

It is one of the most beautiful compensations of life that no man
can sincerely try to help another without helping himself.

RALPH WALDO EMERSON

The year was 1982 and the season had turned from a balmy warm autumn to a freezing cold winter in a matter of hours. Though dreariness was trying to settle in, the day was brightened by the plans I (Annie) had for the evening. Some friends and I were looking forward to "down-time girl-time," and for me that meant a few hours away from the demands of family, which at that time of my life included a husband and two small children. As much as I love my sweet family, I was looking forward to time free from responsibility. I was extra excited and relieved that my husband, Steve, agreed to take on the full impact of "kid duty" while I joined the gang for what was to be an intentionally late evening. I headed out joyfully.

Midway through the fun I was surprised to receive a phone call from Steve. He said, "When it's convenient you might want to think about coming on home. There are a few people here who are cold and hungry, and I don't know what to do with them." He concluded by saying, "I'll explain everything when you get here."

Steve's cryptic message left me wondering what was happening back at our house. My curiosity got the best of me, plus I wanted to respond to Steve's request for help, so I cut my evening short and headed home. As I drove up to the house I was a bit confused. I'd imagined the driveway filled with unfamiliar cars, but there were no additional vehicles parked anywhere I could see. I nervously wondered who was waiting inside and why they needed comfort and joy, which I was expected to provide.

True to Steve's word, as I walked in I found seven strangers talking to him and busily engaging our children with laughter and conversation. Whisking me off to the side, Steve explained. Earlier that evening the kiddos talked him into taking a quick road trip to the local discount store to spend some of their "hard begged" allowance. As he drove into the parking lot he saw what appeared to be a stranded recreational vehicle off to the side. Feeling an inner tug of the "Good Samaritan" spirit, Steve went over to check on the occupants of the home on wheels. He found a Christian singing group whose well-used touring vehicle had broken down and refused to budge another inch. To the beleaguered travelers' relief, Steve was friendly and caring. The songsters were cold, hungry, and devoid of any plan of action. Not being from the area, they didn't know anyone they could call for help. Since it was getting late they'd resigned themselves to spending the night in the cold, immobile RV.

I've often wondered if these folks were really members
of a Christian rock band, or were they members of a
heavenly Rock of Ages band?...Ultimately it doesn't matter
because we were doing the work of God's kingdom.

Immediately Steve's plans for an uneventful excursion to the store with our kids took a totally different direction. He shuttled the marooned musicians to the safety of our cozy-but-small home. Not having a clue what to do with them once he got them there, he did the only thing he could think to do—he called me.

It didn't take long for me to figure out what needed to be done. I assessed that our "chilled to the bone" visitors hadn't had supper. I took a quick look in the pantry to see what was available to feed such a large number of hungry tummies. Money was always a little tight around our house then, and this evening was no different. An unexpected trip to the grocery store wasn't in our budget. Not willing to be stymied by limitations, I decided to attempt a culinary MacGyver. (If you're a television fan and remember the 1980s, you know MacGyver creatively used whatever was handy to get out of various scrapes. His main tools were duct tape and a Swiss army knife.) Opting for one of our family's favorite meals we called "Breakfast at Sundown," I whipped up a batch of pancakes, fried all the eggs we had, and made coffee.

Steve and I got out our extra sheets and blankets to make beds on the floor near the little Franklin-style wood-burning stove that gave off welcoming warmth. Even though we were limited in our resources, we did our best to make our guests feel at home.

The next day Steve took our new friends back to their crippled RV and helped them secure a reputable mechanic. Before midday they were once again on their journey.

I've often wondered if those folks were really members of a Christian rock band or members of a heavenly Rock of Ages band. Were we feeding and housing angels without knowing it? Ultimately it doesn't matter whether they were heavenly angels or not because we were doing the work of God's kingdom—showing His love to the people around us.

Way back then, on that early winter night when I was stirring pancake batter and Steve was preparing pallets on the floor, neither of us fully realized just how solidly on biblical ground we stood. Much later I learned that showing hospitality isn't just a Southern, neighborly thing to do. It's a Christian mandate. Scripture is clear in numerous places that hospitality, especially to strangers, is a godly obligation for *every* believer.

The Cost of Hospitality

Steve and I felt an incredible level of joy assisting the stranded musicians. We still look back at their visit with fond memories. But as satisfying as it was, there was a price tag. When Steve decided to go to the store that evening, he didn't know that the next 24 hours would be spent helping people he didn't know. Shuttling seven band members to and from their broken-down rig, ferrying the leader of the group to the repair shop, and waiting to make sure the locals who did the repairs treated them fairly cost Steve a lot of time, including a day of work.

We also paid a price in convenience. I gave up part of my long-anticipated evening with my friends to answer Steve's call for help. I went home to a houseful of hungry, cold people who needed to be taken care of. With a heart open to serving and loving God, I immediately set about making them comfortable.

Our finances were also hit. We felt the sting of the cash outlay required to house and feed our guests and the cost of a day of Steve's work. Though some would say it was a relatively small expenditure, at that time in our lives our little piggy bank squealed a bit.

The more I learn about serving God, the more I realize that if we want to offer Him something of value, it will not only cost us, but it *should* cost us. My heart cries out with King David as he said, "I will not offer...offerings to the LORD my God which cost me nothing" (2 Samuel 24:24). Resenting the sacrifice of time, convenience, and resources that showing hospitality exacts from us doesn't result in the offering God deserves. Gladly offering to the Lord our gifts of service, time, finances, and schedules honors Him. And those opportunities are often accomplished through hospitality.

The Currency of Courage

Being hospitable may come naturally for some, but others struggle with just the thought of entertaining. The price some folks must pay to experience the joy that comes with hospitality isn't just money but also includes the currency of courage. One of my friends had to overcome her fear of reaching out to others. She confessed one day that she would rather have a root canal on an abscessed tooth without novocaine than invite a family of four over for dessert. She admits to experiencing heart palpitations, sweaty palms, and weak knees at the mere suggestion of entertaining company. Even with her crippling reservations to opening her home's door, she still has a sincere desire to reach out and help people.

As my friend and I talked, we explored what hospitality is all about. True hospitality isn't simply a personality trait or a cultural tradition. While it may be true that some people naturally enjoy showing random manifestations of kindness, others have to develop the joy of helping. Various regions have cultural traditions of hospitality. Living in the South, for example, includes certain expectations when it comes to hosting. Those who live in other parts of the country commonly assume that "Southern hospitality" comes naturally to those of us who speak with a slow drawl and pepper our conversations with "reckons" and "y'alls." While sweet tea, sugar cookies, and grits may seem the apex of Southern culture, those who live above the Mason-Dixon Line aren't off the hook.

Serving people is a spiritual act, a Christian responsibility, no matter what zip code may be on the light bill. Regardless of personality or home address, entertaining others is imperative if we want to obey and live the truths of Scripture.

Hospitality means opening our eyes to those around us who need a warm smile, an outstretched hand, a willing ear.

My friend's eyes lit up as she realized that one way she could overcome her fear of reaching out to others was to see it as a ministry. Placing a new meaning on the ancient command to be hospitable allowed her to deposit some much-needed currency into her bank of courage. Today she is one of the most gifted folks I know when it comes to entertaining.

Webster's dictionary defines hospitality as "the act, practice or quality of receiving and entertaining strangers or guests in a friendly and generous way." Although this sounds like a sweet thing to do, as my hospitality-challenged friend testified, it's not always a natural fit. I once heard a well-known TV evangelist say to her congregation, "I do not like to have people I don't really know over to my house. I'll take you out and pay for a nice meal, but I don't want you to come to my house. I like my own space."

I'm sympathetic regarding how uncomfortable some people feel when asked to show hospitality to strangers, but there is a biblical imperative to consider. Jesus was very clear on this. According to Luke 14:12-14 He said,

> When you give a luncheon or a dinner, do not invite your friends or your brothers or your relatives or rich neighbors, otherwise they may also invite you in return and that will be your repayment. But when you give a reception, invite the poor, the crippled, the lame, the blind, and you will be blessed, since they do not have the means to repay you; for you will be repaid at the resurrection of the righteous.

Was Jesus prohibiting family gatherings in this command? Was He forbidding us to have a Christmas open house and invite our neighbors and friends? Of course not. There are times and occasions when we open our hearts and homes to those we love. Jesus, however, was broadening the definition of hospitality to include people who may normally be invisible to us, who are off our radar, who are easy to forget, or who may even be neglected. And what He said so long ago applies to us now.

If we limit our hospitality to those who make us feel comfortable, to those who can reciprocate with an invitation to their homes, or to those who benefit us in some way, we are the losers. Hebrews 13:2-3 tells us why we are to open our hearts and open our homes to others. Let these words sink into your spirit and boost the intensity of your "want to": "Do not neglect to show hospitality to strangers, for by this some have entertained angels without knowing it. Remember the prisoners, as though in prison with them, and those who are ill-treated, since you yourselves also are in the body."

Hospitality means opening our eyes to those around us who need a warm smile, an outstretched hand, a willing ear. We need to look for opportunities to share hospitality, even wondering, *Who is God going to bring into my life today? What blessing does He have in store through people I haven't met yet?*

An Eternal Reward

Sometimes we get understandably distracted by the endless details of life. Many of the things that consume our time are important and worth the attention they demand. Taking care of our families, working to provide for their physical and financial needs, serving in our churches, and being a light for Christ in civic circles are all good uses of our time and energy. In the midst of the many details we can forget to look beyond the immediate needs of those around us. I've heard this adage so many times, but it's so true: "This is not a dress rehearsal. This is it. We get one go around at this life. Make the most of it." This timeless truth is motivation enough to not overlook our responsibility to serve God through hospitality. When we hotly pursue the privilege of reaching out to others we bring the world into our homes. Strangers and friends expand our experiences in ways we might otherwise miss. We can quickly become isolated and even hardened toward others if we limit our contact with people outside our usual social circle.

Jesus emphasized the importance of practicing deliberate hospitality. He gives us this very familiar warning about keeping ourselves removed from those who are in need and those who are hurting:

> Then the King will say to those on His right, "Come, you who are blessed of My Father, inherit the kingdom prepared for you from the foundation of the world. For I was hungry, and you gave Me something to eat; I was thirsty, and you gave Me something to drink; I was a stranger, and you invited Me

in; naked, and you clothed Me; I was sick, and you visited Me; I was in prison, and you came to Me…Truly I say to you, to the extent that you did it to one of these brothers of Mine, even the least of them, you did it to Me" (Matthew 25:34-36,40).

What was Jesus saying? He was defining hospitality as the hands and feet of love.

This passage goes on to express the consequence of neglecting the opportunity to show hospitality to others: " 'Truly I say to you, to the extent that you did not do it to one of the least of these, you did not do it to Me.' These will go away into eternal punishment, but the righteous into eternal life" (verses 45-46).

Without question, hospitality benefits the one who is in need. As a result of being the hands and feet of hospitality, the famished one no longer aches with hunger pangs. The thirsty one's tongue no longer clings to the roof of his mouth. The stranger has a friend he can call upon. The naked one no longer carries the shame of exposure and humiliation. The infirm now have a chance for recovery and healing. And the one in prison has hope that someone cares if he or she lives or dies. Yes, great and good things are the result as we become the hands and feet of God through serving others. However, the greater good is credited to our accounts for meeting the needs of others. Our hearts are broadened and our lives are enriched as we accept the privilege of giving to those who are in need. "It is more blessed to give than receive" sounds odd but is certainly true.

When we open our homes, we're engaging in the fruit of ministry. Steve and I had the privilege of hosting a couple of ministers from the lovely island of Jamaica. Not only did we benefit from their company, but our hearts were opened to an area of the world where ministry is taking place that we'd never considered. Who benefited the most from this couple staying in our home? I have no doubt Steve and I received more from them than they did with pumpkin bread and chicken casserole. Matthew 10:40-42 reveals Jesus saying,

He who receives you receives Me, and he who receives Me receives Him who sent Me. He who receives a prophet in the name of a prophet shall receive a prophet's reward; and he who receives a righteous man in the name of a righteous man shall receive a righteous man's reward. And whoever in the name of a disciple gives to one of these little ones even a cup of cold water to drink, truly I say to you, he shall not lose his reward.

The importance of seeking out those who find themselves in life's downward spiral helps us see what we really have. My husband is an avid outdoorsman. The hunter's woods are Steve's sanctuary, his counselor's couch, his painter's studio, and his songwriter getaway. Steve has written many books about his outdoor experiences. He uses what he's learned while hunting to teach life lessons to people who share his appreciation for the outdoors. Among those who love the wide-open spaces are men who have been incarcerated. These prisoners, although confined to the indoors, are able to reconnect with the outdoors through Steve's great writing abilities. As a result of Steve's correspondence with them, I've been privileged to go with Steve to visit some of these men. Through visiting, we are taking our hospitality to them. They can't come to us, so we go to them.

When we hear those iron prison doors clang behind us, we're always brought to our knees, figuratively speaking. We're not afraid of those who are behind bars, but we're filled with gratitude for the freedom we enjoy. God's Word tells us to "remember the prisoners, as though in prison with them, and those who are ill-treated, since you yourselves also are in the body."

Whether the pendulum of opportunities to reach out to others swings from inviting someone to our homes or visiting those confined to cells, God has promised an eternal reward for our obedience of being hospitable.

2

Being Joyful Givers

A woman invited her pastor and his family over for Sunday lunch. As the group sat down to eat, the pastor asked the daughter of their host to offer the mealtime blessing. She responded that she didn't know what to say. The pastor replied, "Just pray what you hear your mommy say."

The little girl began to pray, "Oh God, why did I invite all these people over to eat on such a hot day?"

Yes, there are times when giving hospitality makes the needle on our "mumble meter" go further to the right than we care to admit. Nonetheless, the true depth of our character is sometimes best tested when serving others. First Peter 4:9 is more than a subtle reminder of how we are to respond to inviting folks into our home: "Be hospitable to one another without complaint." I'll be the first to admit that on more than one occasion I've bent the needle on the "mumble meter." I remember a time, for example, when Steve invited three people to come and stay at our house during Nashville's Gospel Music Association Week. Ordinarily this wouldn't have been a problem; however, Steve was not only away on a 14-day singing tour but he forgot to tell me about the company coming until just a few hours before they were to arrive!

To add to the stress factor of having guests I wasn't expecting, our oven was on the blink. My only means of baking was a small toaster oven. What did I do? I muttered a bit and then accepted the situation and set about getting ready. I was sure I could make do. I immediately started cooking food for the week.

For some reason everything I made in preparation contained onions. When the three "strangers" arrived, the first thing the wife said was, "Oh, by the way, I'm deathly allergic to onions. The slightest hint of onion and my breathing shuts off."

And that was the beginning of a long week. Did I complain? Of course I did—but not to our guests. On Steve's return we had a very in-depth conversation about communication.

Hospitality Isn't Always Easy

Throughout Scripture we're instructed in what is important in living the Christian life. Romans 12:9-13 lists many godly attitudes and virtues that we are to practice:

> Let love be without hypocrisy.
> Abhor what is evil; cling to what is good.
> Be devoted to one another in brotherly love;
> give preference to one another in honor;
> not lagging behind in diligence,
> fervent in spirit, serving the Lord;
> rejoicing in hope,
> persevering in tribulation,
> devoted to prayer,
> contributing to the needs of the saints,
> practicing hospitality.

Notice in this passage that *practicing hospitality* is listed right along with hating evil, doing good, devoted to prayer, and even giving money to the needy. In the King James Version the words used are "given to hospitality." In the Greek language the precise meaning of *given* is to "aggressively pursue something; to ardently follow after something; or to hotly pursue something until you finally catch it."

Paul describes the pursuit of hospitality as aggressively setting our hearts on the goal of serving through hospitality. Author Rick Renner, in *Sparkling Gems from the Greek,* puts it this way: "Hotly pursue and never stop pursuing the goal of becoming hospitable until you have caught on to the idea of hospitality and have genuinely become a hospitable person."

Genesis 18 shares a great hospitality story. The great patriarch Abraham was sitting in the entrance of his tent in the heat of the day when three men arrived. He immediately got up from the comfort of his chair, ran from the tent door to meet them, bowed down, and entreated them to come in and grant him the *pleasure* of showing them hospitality. He said, "Please let a little water be brought and wash your feet, and rest yourselves under the tree; and I will bring a piece of bread, that you may refresh yourselves" (verses 4-5).

Abraham understood the true spirit of hospitality is giving more than is promised or expected. Instead of going into the tent and grabbing a piece of leftover bread from that morning's baking, he said to Sarah, "Quickly, prepare three measures [20 quarts] of fine flour, knead it and make bread cakes" (verse 6). Abraham was also not content to just give his visitors fresh bread his wife baked. No, he then ran to the herd and took a tender and choice calf, which he gave to a servant who was instructed to "hurry and prepare it." Abraham didn't hesitate to interrupt his leisurely afternoon snooze and the enjoyable cool spot in the entrance of his tent door when company arrived. Setting aside his own comfort, he set into motion a frenzied baking and butchering task. The welfare of his guests was his main concern.

The strangers whom Abraham graciously lavished with hospitality turned out to be messengers from God. After eating the fine meal prepared for them, they blessed Abraham with the news that God was going to open the womb of his wife, Sarah, and grant him an heir even in his advanced age.

The two angels who visited with Abraham then moved on to where his nephew Lot was living. According to the Middle Eastern code of hospitality, when a stranger requested sanctuary in a home the host became responsible for the safety and well-being of the guest. While they were there a mob of godless men from Sodom demanded that

Lot turn the men over to be sexually molested. Lot refused and, in appeasement, offered his daughters in the place of the two visitors. As deplorable and misguided an act as this was, Lot was fulfilling the long-standing and understood cultural law of protecting his guests, even to the detriment of his own daughters.

Another biblical example of hospitality is found in 1 Kings 17. The Lord told His prophet Elijah to go to Zarephath and stay there, and that a widow would provide for him.

> So he arose and went to Zarephath, and when he came to the gate of the city, behold, a widow was there gathering sticks; and…he called to her and said, "Please bring me a piece of bread in your hand." But she said, "As the LORD your God lives, I have no bread, only a handful of flour in the bowl and a little oil in the jar; and behold, I am gathering a few sticks that I may go in and prepare for me and my son, that we may eat it and die." Then Elijah said to her, "Do not fear; go, do as you have said, but make me a little bread cake from it first and bring it to me, and afterward you may make one for yourself and for your son" (verses 9-13).

If you are familiar with this account you know the widow did exactly as the prophet Elijah requested. She showed preference to the prophet and unselfish hospitality even amid her desperate want and deprivation. God rewarded her obedience and generosity of spirit by seeing to it that the little bit of flour and oil lasted until the end of the famine. The widow and her son did not die of starvation.

As I read the account of the widow of Zarephath giving the prophet the food from her table, I thought about the many stories my mother told of her mom. Grandma Naomi birthed my mother in 1921 and raised her during the terrible depression. She raised her six children in a hollow in rural West Virginia and knew what it was like to live in abject poverty. My mother told me that since most of the folks who lived in that area were in the same economically depressed condition, everyone accepted that life was a struggle. Although everyone was scraping by to feed their kids, there was one family in particular who took advantage of my grandmother's tender heart and generous hospitality:

> As sure as the sun would come up in the morning, you could count on this mother bringing all her children to our house at least once a week. They would sit and wait for my mom to fix whatever food she could find. Then, just as the woman expected, mom would invite them all to stay and eat. It was mom who would be the one to go without food. She was so kind and always wanted to be hospitable. The woman and her children would eat their fill and then get up and go home.

When my mom told my siblings and me this part of the story we got terribly angry that grandma was taken advantage of and went without food. My mom then shared what Grandmother Naomi said about the situation: "Don't worry about me. Remember, there's always someone worse off than us. I feel sorry for her. She's just trying to feed her children."

Hospitality seems to be the biblical litmus test of whether or not a person has a servant's heart.

My grandmother took the Word of God to heart and lived its principles without complaint. In Romans 12:20 it says, "If your enemy is hungry, feed him, and if he is thirsty, give him a drink." If we are to treat our enemies with grace and generosity, how much more are we to show our friends and neighbors acts of hospitality! Grandma could see that her neighbor wasn't her enemy, only a desperate woman. Truly, it takes a devoted, godly heart to get that good at hospitality!

God's emphasis on hospitality is also evident in His guidelines for Christian leaders. Consider these instructions:

- "An overseer [church leader], then, must be above reproach, the husband of one wife, temperate, prudent, respectable, *hospitable*, able to teach" (1 Timothy 3:2).

- "The overseer must be...*hospitable*, loving what is good, sensible, just, devout, self-controlled" (Titus 1:7-8).

Should we find it curious that hospitality is among the qualifications God required as a test of eligibility for Christian leadership? No. Hospitality seems to be the biblical litmus test of whether a person has a servant's heart. It was true then, and it applies today as well.

Most of us know these familiar verses: "The greatest among you will be your servant. For whoever exalts himself will be humbled, and whoever humbles himself will be exalted" (Matthew 23:11-12). A true host will be the first up in the morning and the last to go to bed at night in order to serve. Hospitality is the ultimate demonstration of love for one another. God's servants are great role models for others by being willing to meet the basic needs of people they come into contact with. True hospitality keeps our hearts open and bent toward the most hurting, the most needy in God's kingdom. The hungry, the thirsty, the lonely, the naked, the imprisoned, the hurting are to be the focus of ministry and hospitality. These are the people who make up the body of Christ.

The Flip Side

Even as hospitality shows the goodness of a person's servant heart, lack of hospitality is very telling. In Luke 7:44-47 we read how an opportunity to show hospitality was wasted and demonstrated an absence of the attitude of service.

> Turning toward the woman, [Jesus] said to Simon, "Do you see this woman? I entered your house; you gave Me no water for My feet, but she has wet My feet with her tears and wiped them with her hair. You gave Me no kiss; but she, since the time I came in, has not ceased to kiss My feet. You did not anoint My head with oil, but she anointed My feet with

perfume. For this reason I say to you, her sins, which are many, have been forgiven, for she loved much; but he who is forgiven little, loves little."

Simon's lack of hospitality showed an ungrateful, unloving heart. Without question he committed several social mistakes. It was a common courtesy in those days to wash (or have a servant wash) a guest's sand-covered feet as a "welcome to our house" gesture. Simon also failed to offer another appropriate greeting, which was a kiss in those days. The undercurrent of Simon's hard character was exposed by his lack of consideration. In contrast, the woman who performed the humbling act of foot washing, who had many flaws and had made many mistakes in her life, was forgiven because of the humility she displayed through the graciousness she showed Jesus.

The Heart of Hospitality

To find the true essence of practicing hospitality it is important to understand and embrace the truths found in Matthew 5. Jesus' teaching called the people of that day to a Christian walk that was uncomfortable and unnatural. In essence He said that all who follow Him must be willing to become "Second Milers." If they were asked to go one mile, they were to willingly do so and then go a second mile. True hospitality is going further than required and giving more than expected.

Jesus had already stirred up a boatload of trouble when he said to the mostly Jewish audience, "Do not resist an evil person; but whoever slaps you on your right cheek, turn the other to him also. If anyone wants to sue you and take your shirt, let him have your coat also" (verses 39-40).

To appreciate the impact of this directive, it helps to understand that Jewish law stated that a man could sue someone and, in payment for winning the case, he could take the man's tunic as part of the settlement. However, the law would not allow the man who won the lawsuit to take the defendant's cloak. The cloak or outer garment was sometimes used as a form of shelter—a tent—if the man needed to sleep outside. What Jesus was saying to those listening that day on a mountainside was, "Go beyond what is required by the law and let love become the measuring stick for your behavior." As if that wasn't enough challenge to the norm, He had the audacity to add, "Whoever forces you to go one mile, go with him two" (verse 41).

If we "moderns" shake our heads and ask, "How are we supposed to live like that?" just think how difficult those teachings were for the folks there. At the time Israel was occupied by the Romans. A Roman soldier could walk up to any Jewish man or boy and, without regard to what that person was doing or where he was going, demand that the Jew go with him and carry his belongings for one mile. Supposedly Jewish fathers took their sons out and walked one mile. The goal was to teach them the exact distance so they wouldn't walk one foot farther than the law demanded. This law of enslavement infuriated every Jew and inflamed hatred toward the soldiers and the government of Rome. When Jesus said, "Don't just walk one mile, but go ahead and carry the load two miles," He greatly offended His audience. Those who believed Jesus to be the Messiah, the King of all Jews, must have been sorely disheartened to think that not only was Jesus refusing to immediately deliver them from the iron fist of Rome, but He was actually asking them to go beyond what was demanded of them in their powerless servitude.

Within this "second mile" mentality is the true spirit of hospitality. As Christ followers we are to go beyond what is required and give more than is expected. Just as Abraham offered his guests a piece of bread and then prepared a feast, we are to give generously.

This hospitality goal is noble in theory, but it can be very hard to live out. One particular instance about giving and then having to give even more comes to mind. While our family was traveling on one of our many road trips (we sing for a living), we decided to take a little excursion and attend a Saturday afternoon outdoor rally sponsored by a Christian radio station. While we were munching our cotton candy and drinking our lemonade we were privileged to meet a sweet family of seven. We talked for a while and then, as we parted, Steve said, "If you're ever in Nashville be sure to come see us."

Fast-forward about six months. I woke up one morning and had a keen sense that I should cook extra food that day. I thought at first it was some sort of nesting urge that goes along with being pregnant. Then I began to wonder, *Is the Lord prompting me to prepare for company?* Believing (and hoping) that it was the latter and wanting to be obedient, I cooked most of the morning, got beds ready, and waited. About two o'clock I thought about all the food I'd prepared and decided I'd totally misunderstood the urge. I figured I should invite some folks over for dinner.

Each person I called was busy and couldn't come. I thought, *Well, I must have just been imagining what I thought I heard.* Around four o'clock I got a call. It was the family we'd met at the festival a few months earlier. They asked if they could come and stay with us. I eagerly responded, "Your supper is ready and your beds are made!"

While I'm not always so open, I was excited that I'd heard and obeyed the Lord. After six days of having an additional family in our tiny house the thrill was waning. The worst moment was when they asked if they could give our home address as a forwarding address for their mail.

Steve and I were scheduled to leave for a concert trip in a couple of days, and I had yet to get ready. Taking care of our company had worn me out. It was terribly awkward to ask them how long they were planning on staying and let them know our expectations.

Feeling a bit guilty for asking our company to leave, I was determined to send them off with clean clothes, fresh bedding, and bellies full of food. I took the mother to a Laundromat and made sure all their clothes were clean. We took them to our church, and the people there gave them money for food and gas. On the day they were to go, Steve and I took them to a local restaurant that had a breakfast buffet. They ate until their tummies couldn't hold another bite. Then we took them back to our house so they could get an early start.

They stood around and talked. For three hours they talked. Before long it was time for lunch. By this time, quite honestly, my good feelings were gone. I was getting angry and was ready to scream, "Enough already! Get out of here!"

Earlier that morning I'd prepared an envelope for each of the children. Inside I put a $5 bill. I thought the parents might take the money for food or gas, so I planned on asking if it would be possible for the children to use the money for a special treat or toy. As the morning dragged on, my children started asking about lunch. I told them to be quiet. I wasn't going to cook one more meal for our guests. I figured the family had their chance to leave with their appetites satisfied, and I wasn't about to start pulling more food out for lunch. (Our budget was tight, and food was expensive.) My growing ire also prompted me to not give the children the money after all. I tucked the little envelopes away because I decided I'd given enough. I was not being a "hilarious giver." Instead, I was feeling like an easy mark.

I wish I could go back and do it right. But the Lord
is gracious, and I've been given many opportunities
since then to develop and give true hospitality.

Finally our company reluctantly started the leaving process. As they were departing, the little children reached into their pop-up camper and pulled out the only book they owned and gave it to our children, Nathan and Heidi. Needless to say, the children's overflowing generosity in spite of their poverty made me feel like pond scum. All the horrible things I secretly thought about them were replaced with sadness for their situation.

With crow feathers sticking out of the sides of my mouth I said, "Oh, wait a minute! I have something for you kids too." I quickly went inside and retrieved the envelopes I'd prepared for them.

As they drove off I felt ashamed because I'd failed the "second mile" test. I started out great, doing fine on that first mile, but then I really fizzled on the next one. After much thought, I came to better understand why the people in Jesus' day had such a hard time with His teachings. But I also realized an important truth. The first mile was something they were forced to do. But on the second mile they became the masters because they chose to go further.

I'm not quite sure when I began to feel like a slave to that family that showed up at our door and their lingering presence became more than I cared to tolerate. But because I only managed a "first mile" attitude, I never knew the joy of becoming the master of the situation. Sadly, I didn't get to experience the true heart of hospitality that time.

I wish I could go back and relive that time again…and do it right. But that's not going to happen. But the Lord is gracious, and I've been given many opportunities since then to develop and give true hospitality.

3

Give...but Be Wise

Before we go deeper into the subject of hospitality, I want to add a warning: If you feel an eagerness to obey God in the area of entertaining, be listening to Him and let Him tell you when to temper your enthusiasm with a bold willingness to refuse entry to those who might bring harm into your home or life. Not everyone who asks to come in should be permitted to do so. Be wise as you exercise your gift of hospitality that is needed so desperately by those who are "unaware angels."

A good illustration of the need to be a discerning host was offered by a close acquaintance. In our circle of friends she is well-known for being quick and fearless at showing hospitality to strangers and just about anyone in need. However, the wide-open door to her heart was necessarily pushed closed by an awkward situation she and her husband encountered.

For about a year the two of them had been trying to help a couple who were having marital difficulties. They spent many hours of their time listening, counseling, and instructing the struggling husband and wife on ways to reconcile their differences and surrender their lives and marriage to the Lord. Sadly, most of their advice went unheeded and eventually the couple separated. One day while my friend and her husband were visiting the local jail, ministering to someone in need, they came upon the husband they had counseled. My friends were surprised to learn that he'd been incarcerated for a serious breach of the law. The troubled man explained that he could be released from jail if he could find a responsible person willing to take him in. He asked if he could go home with them and stay for a while.

Not everyone who asks to come in should
be permitted to do so. Be wise.

My friend and her husband conferred and agreed that it didn't seem like a wise thing to do. They refused the man's request. When they said no, the man exploded in rage and had to be subdued by attending officers. Because he'd made it quite clear that he was a danger to himself as well as to others, my friends knew he was exactly where he needed to be. They'd made the right decision. Ever since then my friend seeks discerning wisdom when it comes to opening their home.

"No" Can Be Appropriate

Examples of when to say no when someone asks, "May I come in?" are endless. The following account shows how easy it is to fall into "good intentions gone bad."

For several weeks there were several men working at a friend's house. One of the guys was a recently divorced man. He'd proven to be very friendly and helpful during the project. She had many decisions that had to be made, and he'd given several suggestions that made the task go more smoothly. She felt very fortunate to have him on her "team" of workmen. Several days into the job he very politely asked if he could come by and watch the "big game" on the next Sunday afternoon. He knew that she and her family had a high-definition, wide-screen television with surround sound. He said he didn't want to watch the game alone in his small apartment on his less-than-impressive TV. Feeling sorry for him and his sad state of affairs, she agreed and said he could come by. But in her heart something didn't feel quite right.

She admitted, "I was honestly trying to be a Christian witness to the men by blessing them from time to time with fresh-baked cookies and hot coffee. I always tried to have kind words for them as they worked. I feared that I would appear unloving or selfish if I refused the guy's request to come over, so I said yes. But the moment I said that he could join us for the game, the red light of suspicion started blinking in my heart. My husband would be at work that day, but I thought it would be all right because the house would be filled with our children and their friends. Still, the warning light kept blinking." Unfortunately, feeling too awkward about changing her mind, she didn't tell him not to come.

When she told me her story later she was still upset with what happened that Sunday afternoon. Not wanting to appear rude toward her worker/guest, she sat in the living room watching the ball game with the man. She was not at all interested in the game so she leafed through a magazine. Suddenly the suspicion that she had errantly extended an invitation to the man was confirmed. Out of the blue he said, "How 'bout I come over there and rub your shoulders?"

Without a micromoment of hesitation she jumped up and said, "Buster, the game is over! It's time for you to leave." As she shared this with me, the tremble in her voice revealed her agitation. "I thought it would be awkward if I refused his request to watch the game with us. Boy was I wrong! It was ten times more awkward after that to have him working around the house. I couldn't wait for the project to be over. While I got a nice remodel job, I also gained something even more important. I got a kick in the 'don't be so stupid' pants. That mistake is something I won't make again. Next time the red light starts blinking on the dash of my heart, I won't ignore it!"

Being Discerning Isn't Rude

The ancient attitudes and rules about hospitality that existed in Bible times recognized the inherent dangers that a host can face.

For that reason the policies more often benefited those who opened their doors to others rather than those who walked through them. For example, it was customary for those who were passing through a town to not go to someone's door seeking lodging. Instead they knew to go to a local open place or gathering spot, such as a water well or city gate, and wait. Knowing it was considered a dishonor to a community if a stranger was uninvited to someone's home before nightfall, the travelers anticipated an invitation. But included in that known rule was the caveat of screening those who waited. This safety measure made it possible for a host to not worry about who would be coming.

This screening custom would have been a good one for one teacher we knew who lived and taught at a college in a southern Tennessee town. She had a heart for the "broken vessels" who sat at the desks in her classroom. This woman often invited them into her home to spend time and share a nice meal and warm conversation. One of the students who benefited from her excellent teaching skills and warm personality was our son, Nathan.

Our hearts were shredded the day he called home to tell us that one of the students she befriended had murdered her in her own home. We were brokenhearted by the senseless waste of such a precious person. Those who loved her agreed she should have been more careful. However, most of her friends conceded to the good possibility that if given the same opportunity to be the hands of love for the young people she cared so much for, she wouldn't have changed a thing. Still, the students who suffered losing their teacher departed the school with a seed of caution planted in their hearts regarding being hospitable—but staying safe. I'm sure this lesson will serve them as well.

We made the decision that we would be more
careful about who we invited into our home.

Quite a while ago Steve and I experienced the importance of being careful while caring. The first year we were married we decided to reach out to the homeless in our area. For Thanksgiving dinner I scraped up as much money as I could and bought a small turkey and prepared the side dishes that go with a traditional holiday dinner. While I was cooking, Steve took our old 1950 mint-green Chevy out to look for people on the streets who had no place to go. Scripturally speaking, he went "out into the highways and along the hedges, and [compelled] them to come in" to dine with us (Luke 14:23). When Steve returned home from his mission, I watched as six scruffy men crawled out of the car. I immediately worried about the tiny amount of food I'd prepared. There was no way, humanly speaking, that the skinny little turkey sitting on the kitchen counter was going to fill those empty stomachs. We were going to need a miracle for the men to be satisfied.

As we began our meal, we asked the men if they would bow their heads with us and ask God to bless the food. I silently added my own little prayer that God would do something akin to what He did when He multiplied the loaves and fishes and fed more than 5,000 people (Matthew 14). Perhaps the men looking at our humble table of food were praying something similar. To my astonishment, I was blessed to find that at the end of a veritable feeding frenzy we had food left over!

As the turkey was being reslaughtered, we learned some interesting details about the men who had their feet under our table. One of them, the youngest of the six, had a particularly disturbing past. During the meal he entertained us with accounts of his time in the "big house." He told us how he learned to make flashlights, liquor, weapons, and other "useful" items during his "unfortunate" incarcerations. For some reason he seemed harmless enough in our presence. But when he left, he literally went from our house, out onto the Nashville streets, and murdered a woman a few blocks away. The last meal he experienced as a free man was at our table!

As I think back over that unforgettable Thanksgiving, I still get shivers up my spine. I'm glad we showed hospitality toward those homeless men that day, but we also made the decision to be more careful after that, especially when we had children at home. I urge you to do the same.

4

Throwing Your Heart Open

*H*ome doesn't seem like a big enough word considering all that it encompasses. Home is:

- a place where we feel safest, even though the worst is known about us
- a launching pad
- a safe harbor
- a lighthouse
- an emergency room
- a sanctuary yet comedy central
- a counselor's couch and a coffee shop
- a penitentiary at times, even though it's where we learn to spread our wings and fly
- a beauty shop
- a rescue mission
- a detention center
- a soup kitchen
- a preschool
- a place where we learn how much we don't know
- a warm spot and, rarely, sometimes a cold shoulder
- Saturday morning pancakes

- popcorn for supper
- usually safe, but sadly sometimes dangerous
- a place you can't wait to get away from
- a place you can't wait to get back to
- a physical place that can lose its hold on your heart when those who once lived there are gone
- ultimately home is love with windows and doors

In this complex and private residence we are mandated by God to open the doors wide and allow others, even strangers, in. Hospitality is sharing the goodness of our homes with others. It is the most intimate of dwellings and yet God asks that we make it the most accessible place possible.

Through Eyes of Hospitality

This past summer I was privileged to host a "cousins weekend." Being born and raised in a small community in West Virginia, I lived just over the hill from my cousin Barbara Jane. We were less than a month apart in age, and our fathers were brothers in every sense of the word. Our mothers were also fast friends. Growing up together, Barbara and I shared a love of music and a soul bond that can only be forged by bloodline and years of togetherness. It was sheer joy to see my sweet cousin and dear friend after much time apart. I was amazed at how quickly our friendship picked up right where it had left off years before. It was as though time had stood still, and we were still young women facing an exciting yet frightening world together.

My other visiting cousin, Mary Jean, lived up the road about five miles from where I lived. Our fathers were also brothers, and my mother regarded Aunt Maxine, Mary's mother, as closer than a sister. Mary and I shared our long-term dreams, our most cherished secrets, and our love of baking cookies. On one of our many adventures, we even got marooned in a rowboat and had to be rescued. Although we weren't in any real danger, it was quite dramatic for two highly imaginative teenagers. Those kind of experiences have a way of cementing friends together for life. In fact, Mary Jean is the one who signed the marriage certificate as a witness when Steve and I got married.

Barbara Jane, Mary Jean, and I came from large families. As a result, we had built-in best friends from the beginning. Our reunion was joyful! We were three grandmas spending a weekend remembering our childhoods and rekindling friendships that had been sorely neglected due to a decade of time, demands of families, and distance.

As close as we were, there was a notable difference in how we were raised. While mom and dad worked harder than two people should ever have to work, our house was not what they wanted for their large family. I was raised in a small, four-room house with an outside toilet until I was a teenager. My cousins were raised in what I regarded as large, beautiful homes. The one thing I remember most about their houses was the indoor plumbing!

Hospitality is using what we have to make others feel welcomed and cherished. I challenge you to swing your hearts and doors open and let your love flow.

While we were reminiscing I suddenly realized that although Barbara and Mary spent the night at my house many, many times, I didn't remember our visits the same way they did. I was more fixated on the amenities we didn't have rather than seeing what we really did possess. As my cousins shared their recollections of spending nights in our tiny house, they recounted fondly the adventurous midnight treks to the outhouse. They didn't seem to remember the cramped sleeping arrangements that had to accommodate six siblings and an extra cousin or two. As they detailed their memories of our sleepovers, my eyes filled with tears. They recalled the beautiful clarity of my mother's voice as she sang the wonderful old hymns from her childhood and played the piano. They relived the smell of my mom's famous cherry pies and the laughter that rang out as she told colorful stories of growing up in the "hollers" of West Virginia. They remembered my father's sweet demeanor and spontaneous laugh.

The conversations with Mary and Barbara helped me realize how my mother and father were more than willing to open their hearts and doors wide to make their small house a hub of fun, food, and happiness. It wasn't until I saw my childhood home through the eyes of my cousins that I was able to realize I'd been wealthy beyond compare. My mother knew the true meaning of extending hospitality. She realized it's all about using what we have to make others feel welcomed and cherished. That's a goal I have as I give hospitality and make wonderful memories for everyone who walks through my door.

Having a small house or not having the niceties we desire is no excuse for closing our doors to those around us. I challenge you to swing your hearts and doors open and let love flow in and out of your homes.

5

Ready or Not— Here They Come!

There's a humorous story that's been floating around for a long time, but no matter how many times I hear it, it still tickles my funny bone. A new pastor went out to visit some parishioners. At one of the houses there were cars in the driveway and a light on in the front room. However, after knocking on the door several times, there was no response. So the pastor took out his business card and wrote on the back, "Behold, I stand at the door and knock. If anyone hears my voice and opens the door, I will come in (Revelation 3:20)." He stuck the card in the door and left.

When the offering plate was passed the next Sunday the pastor found that his card had been returned. Written just below the message he had penned was, "I heard the sound of You in the garden, and I was afraid for I was naked (Genesis 3:10)."

Most of us would like to be ready for company 100 percent of the time, but sooner or later an unexpected visitor will show up and catch us unprepared. There have been times when the "out of the blue" visitor has seen my red face of embarrassment. Even worse, others at my door have witnessed the ashen look that says, "Just shoot me!" How can we effectively provide "drop of a hat" hospitality?

Steve's mama was a genuine pro at being an "instant in season" host. She was good at it because she had plenty of practice through the years. And that practice came with her role as wife of a pastor at a church that had several regular attendees who drove considerable distances to town from their homes deep in the country to attend Sunday morning service. If they also planned to attend evening service, instead of driving all the way home and back again that night, some opted to stay in town. And guess where they'd tend to congregate.

Lillian's goal was to never cause her guests to feel unwanted by sensing that she was stressed and unnerved by their presence. She knew if the "sheep" felt welcome and safe it would deepen the impact of her ministry.

According to Steve, it's hard to number the times the Chapman family of four would gather at their Sunday midday lunch table only to hear a knock at the door. He said his mother, Lillian, learned to never be surprised by those knocks and, in fact, would often prepare extra biscuits and toss a few added drumsticks into the frying pan "just in case." He also recalls that his mother would even do a little extra cleaning prior to the busy Sunday activities so she wouldn't have to scramble to make the house presentable if folks suddenly appeared at their front door.

I struggle to be as consistently gracious as Lillian. Thankfully, these days we have portable instant-advance-notice devices called cellular phones that people use to give "a fair warning" of their arrival.

Lillian's willingness to swing the hospitality door wide was made much more enjoyable by being prepared physically and mentally for unexpected guests. The physical part of readiness is not that complicated really. Most of us know how to make a house presentable by straightening up a little and putting a few things away. It's the mental preparedness that is the greater challenge, and that's where Lillian shined! Her attitude was shaped by her goal of never causing her guests to feel unwanted by sensing that she was stressed and unnerved by their presence. She knew that if the "sheep" felt welcome and safe in their home it would deepen the impact of her ministry.

The warm feelings Lillian generated in her visitors were quite the opposite from what my sister and her family experienced during a much-needed vacation to Ireland. They loved everything about their trip except one memorable glitch. They stayed two days at a "bed and breakfast" operated by a couple in a small village. Unfortunately the husband forgot to tell his wife they were coming! Upon my sister's family's arrival, the woman didn't try to hide her irritation at being inconvenienced by guests she didn't expect or want. My sister said, "We felt terribly unwelcome but had a huge dilemma. We had no other place to go." They tried to find other accommodations in the tiny town but there was none to be found. They were stuck and felt like complete imposers. It was a miserable time in their journey, to say the least.

Have you been in a situation where you showed up at someone's house without giving advance notice and yet felt totally welcome? Didn't it feel good? But if you've experienced the opposite reception, as my sister and her family did, then you know how awkward it can be. And those uncomfortable feelings our guests sense when we are frazzled and overwrought write negative notes in their memories about their time with us. And sadly, this note is not easily erased.

The good news is it doesn't have to be that way. There are some things we can do that will help us enjoy unannounced, and sometimes even self-invited guests and make them feel good about their visit.

First Things First

Being God's hands of love on a moment's notice is a wonderful and worthy desire to have. But we have to keep in mind that it's a big goal made up of a lot of small, daily disciplines. Mopping floors, scrubbing commodes, and putting away the dishes may not sound like spiritual activities, but they are. The key to keeping a house in a state of preparedness for the "drive by" guest is doing two things on a regular basis: cleaning and limiting clutter.

Cleaning It Up and Keeping the Clutter Down

I once heard a preacher say, "Some of you want to take authority over demons and devils and yet you haven't even taken authority over the dirty dishes in your sink or the piles of laundry waiting to be washed." That astute observation came home to me one day when I was reading a biography of one of God's great servants. I was deeply inspired by William Wilberforce's incredible feats of faith. He relentlessly fought and helped win the war against the enslavement of hundreds of thousands of fellow human beings in England. His long battle with the powers that be and the powers of darkness spanned decades and is a great lesson in perseverance.

I came away from reading his story feeling humbled by all this man did to change his world. However, it's important to remember his acts of nobility were the result of his willingness to invest in the everyday brand of obedience to God. His private life of intense closet prayer and faithful Bible study each day qualified him to be used of God in a great and public way.

Being God's hands of love is a wonderful and worthy desire, but keep in mind that it's a big goal made up of small, daily disciplines. Mopping floors, scrubbing commodes, and putting away the dishes may not sound like spiritual activities, but they are.

The same is true when it comes to offering hospitality. Some of us want to entertain angels, or at least a dignitary or two, yet we forget that those privileges first start by doing those tasks that more than likely go unacknowledged and are perhaps unappreciated by others.

There's an encouraging truth I try to remember when I'm doing the mundane chores to keep my house in "prepared for the unplanned" condition. When I tend to jobs such as occasionally cleaning cobwebs from the light fixtures or dusting the baseboards, I keep in mind that ultimately I'm not doing it for my yet-to-arrive guests. Nor am I doing it for my own glory. Instead, there's a higher purpose: "Whatever you do, do your work heartily, as for the Lord rather than for men" (Colossians 3:23).

With the goal of pleasing the Lord as the most important motivator, perhaps you won't find it drudgery to do what is necessary to get your residence ready—and keep it ready—for "drop in" guests. In fact, with the Lord's pleasure as your chief concern, you might even find the joy that is hinted at in the word *heartily* in the verse. How else on this planet, or in the universe for that matter, can we find joy in doing menial tasks? Truly, it's only by being convinced that we work for a heavenly *Employer of One!*

With that high and noble truth in mind, I suggest a very practical approach to be prepared. Speaking from experience, I can say this idea can accomplish more than almost anything else in terms of making your residence appear presentable and inviting. This activity will provide immediate, noticeable results and foster confidence that will help you not hesitate to open the hospitality door. I'm speaking of decluttering.

While a house may be clean, if there is visible clutter it may appear at first glance to be messy. Whether you're ill, pregnant, working too many hours, discouraged by lots of little or big messes in your house, or just overwhelmed with everything that demands your attention, take heart!

Time to Take Charge

First, buy large, strong garbage bags. Select the room nearest the front door to begin the decluttering process. Remove *all items* you no longer use. I'm not suggesting you get rid of great-grandma's cookie jar or Aunt Sally's crocheted bedspread. Some items have value beyond their usability. But how about taking a second look at the candleholder you bought at the neighbor's yard sale or the yellowed and dusty silk flowers from your sister's wedding? If you're like most of us, there may be several items that take up space, collect dust, and have no real sentimental or monetary value.

If you are one of those individuals who have great difficulty letting go of any items that have become part of your domestic landscape, I have an additional suggestion. Invite a trusted friend over to help you! Make sure the person you bring into your clutter-world knows how to be supportive, firm, and enjoys the challenge of weeding out "unwanted" or "unneeded" treasures.

Now that you've gathered the "extras," pitch them, donate them, or eBay them. Don't leave the room without at least two removable garbage bags of clutter.

To keep the job low-key, take one room at a time, complete the task, and then repeat this process in the next room at a later time. Over a week's time you will have significantly reduced the clutter mess in your house. I loved the liberating feeling of being set free from the bondage of excessive amounts of belongings after I finished this decluttering process. Now Steve and I don't feel so crowded. Clutter not only looks bad in our rooms but it can make us feel even worse because of the constant messiness we know should be dealt with.

Imagine what your physical body would be like if you continued to eat and never eliminated waste. Without question, if you failed to get rid of the "used manna" (as Steve calls it) you would become unhealthy, bloated, and eventually dead from the buildup of toxins and disease. In the same manner, think of all the things you bring into your house each time you come home from shopping. If you're like me, you probably make several trips from the trunk of the car to your house bringing in all the items purchased. After a few times at the grocery store or the local discount mart, every nook and cranny of our houses can be filled with stuff. Since our bodies have an "in and out" system that keeps things running smoothly, it makes perfect sense that our homes would also benefit greatly by an "in and out" system. We will never be able to keep our houses orderly, clean, and beautiful if we fail to purge. Even things that were once cherished eventually might be rendered unneeded and unnecessary.

Here are some additional suggestions courtesy of several people who responded to an unofficial survey I conducted:

- Taking it one room at a time, I enter the room imagining that I'm a guest. I look for what I would think would be clutter to them. Magazines, books, loose papers, and clothes that aren't put away are usually the main culprits on the floor or stacked on desks or table. I sort through the items and make three piles and give those piles titles:

  Toss It Pile
  Give It Away Pile
  Keep It Pile

  And by all means the most important step in this process is to do what the titles demand.

- If I need to quickly make a room "company ready" I've learned to be careful not to get off task. As I clean the surfaces that are visible and eliminate those dust-gathering piles of items that are an eyesore and in the way, I might discover another job that needs to be done. My tendency is to go ahead and do it even though I know that job can wait. While it might be tempting to start pulling out dresser drawers and emptying closets and reorganizing Christmas decorations, I know I have to fight the urge and focus on the task at hand—to make the room presentable. The benefit is that I'm less frazzled, and even more important, the energy that is needed for having company is reserved.

- A couple of years ago I came to grips with the fact that I had way too many books. Not only did the excess of books result in a ton of clutter, the floor of our attic was literally sagging under the weight of the volumes. Realizing that I must do something for the sake of the appearance, as well as the structural integrity of our home, I took the bull by the horns and started the book sorting process. My criteria for keeping or eliminating a book was simple. If the book could be used for reference or research, it was a keeper. However, if I had read the book and knew I would never read it again, it went into my "give it" pile. I ended up taking 20 boxes of books to our church for the library. Now that my "library" has been seriously downsized, I feel much better about people dropping by.

- There's one thing I do often that might seem a little obsessive to some but it helps my confidence level in terms of keeping my house company ready. I go into a room and look up. Sometimes what I find is something I've seen in other homes that makes me say to myself, *They definitely didn't know I was coming.* It's the cobwebs and spider webs that I speak of. To get rid of them I take a broom and fasten a cotton cloth on the bristles. Then I "sweep" the corners of the room at ceiling level. And while I'm working overhead I go ahead and dust the ceiling fan and light fixtures.

- Out of sight dirt leaves a musty, less-than-fresh smell in the house. As the occupants of the home, we may not notice the offensive smells, but they will not get by the unseasoned nose of a guest. For that reason, I thoroughly dust a room at least once a week.

- A long time ago a good friend told me, "If you get caught by surprise with company coming and you're short on time do two things: Make sure your guest bath is clean and clean your kitchen." I liked that suggestion and have remembered it all these years.

- No matter how hard I try to keep my house company ready, I know there are unattractive "blind spots" seen by other people. Why do I know this? Because I've been in homes that were perfect, except for that "one thing." I remember going to a lady's house who was teaching a Bible study for all the young moms in our church. I was excited when she invited us over to her home for our first study. She and her husband were wealthy so I was anxious to see her home with all its beautiful furnishings and maybe get some great ideas on how to decorate my little four room duplex where we were living. We gathered in her home, and just as I had suspected, it was a beautiful display of good taste. I recalled a lot about that afternoon, but one thing I noticed that I'm sure she didn't intend. As lovely as her house was, I noted that at the end of her kitchen island was a well-used trash can. Smeared all the way down the side of the island cabinet were splashes of food. The residue of garbage that had missed its mark looked like it had been there a while. I'm sure she didn't see it or she would have attended to it.

Knowing how memorable her apparent oversight was for me, I determined to look for my own. The solution I came up with was to ask a friend, a good one who would be candid with me, to help me see my own blind spots. I will be forever grateful for my friend's honest help. The blind spot she helped me see has fur, four paws, and a propensity to emit things that smell really bad. The furry friend is still with me, but I've learned how to take care of the "blind spots" that she makes!

6

Cheap or Chic?

I think I (Heidi) was born with a desire for luxurious living. The joke around our home in my growing-up years was that I was secretly adopted from the famous and wealthy Rockefeller Family. I was known to give occasional support to that joke. When I was a mere eight years old, after our family had lunch with some folks who, in my young opinion, had a palatial palace for a house, I made a bold announcement to my parents on the way back to our home: "It's time for us to move to a bigger and nicer home." I wasn't brought up to think so covetously, but wanting the finer things of life seems to be instinctual. Perhaps it's one of the hazards of being human. A few years later, when I was earning a degree in interior design, the research I had to do fanned the "finer" flame of desire. I spent many hours reading decorating magazines and mentally planning my own palatial palace.

Yes, I love pretty things. Time and age haven't erased my desire to be related to the Rockefellers. When we travel, my desire for overnight accommodations is a Ritz Carlton Hotel. While my mind and body would enjoy the luxury, the frugal voice of reason screams "Microtel." Though I have a Ritz Carlton fantasy (and while I'm there I'll visit Tiffany's), I'm fully aware that my pocketbook is—well, let's just say it's not Chanel. Wisdom has taught me that I must discover how to satisfy my "Rockefeller instinct" without spending a fortune.

Can you relate? What I've found is that learning how to make "cheap look chic" isn't the first step in being a good steward of finances. I needed to know *why* to budget and be responsible with my money.

So my journey began. The *why* of the matter has three distinct parts: duty, personal, and spiritual.

Duty

The first reason that motivates me to not overspend is that I love my family, and part of my job as a wife and mom is to be concerned for their welfare. My children seem to have an annoying need to eat, and then there's the unreasonable desire my husband has for not going barefoot to work. Since I love them, I willingly use my imagination and consciously look for creative ways to fulfill my yearning for chic.

With my willing cooperation (and perhaps a smidgen of kicking and screaming), my husband and I decided to stick to a budget. We have earmarked specific amounts of money for everything from groceries to car repairs. Included in the distribution of funds is a small decorating budget for items ranging from new candles to antique urns. I know if I spend over the designated amount, I'm cutting into the money we're saving every month for emergencies, big ticket items, and the future. So I use the funds carefully. Because our home is already filled with plenty of furniture, there's little space for adding bigger items, which is a real advantage. I use the decorating allowance for occasionally upgrading and adding smaller, more refined touches, such as high-quality candles and fresh flowers.

I'm also looking forward, knowing that with two young kids, Emmitt and I are going to need the money we're saving now.

Personal

I know it may sound silly or even sad, but I was well into my twenties before I realized that making *and* saving money are the keys to having money. This concept is ancient and probably common sense, but the truth had to work its way through my Rockefeller attitude. The good news is that I've discovered that "cheap can be chic" if done right. The result is savings, and with the amount saved, I can wisely buy more. What a deal!

Here's how it works. If I want to buy a decorative pillow for my settee, I go to a TJ Maxx or Marshalls store. They have beautiful things for a discounted price. There I can get a pillow plus a throw for the price of one pillow at high-end shops. I don't need to have the most pricey pillow, just one that looks good.

I find it thrilling to see how much I can do with relatively little money. The curtains in my dining room are from Target. They look like raw silk, which is one of my favorite fabrics, but they aren't. The fact that they look silky is good enough for me. The look and style of the curtains are what I'm concerned about. I have friends who have spent ten times as much as I did for window treatments, and theirs don't look that different from mine!

Yes, it's a challenge to live within our means, but it is worth every penny not spent to know we're doing what God wants us to do—be good stewards of what He's provided.

For pure fun I imagine what a haul I could make with the money they spent. What a spending spree! Enjoy it with me—beautiful curtains; a big, fluffy couch; brocaded ottoman; classy end tables; brushed nickel lamps; framed original art; luxuriant pillows; overstuffed chairs; and a soft, wool rug...maybe two rugs...no, make it three! Wasn't that fun? Getting more bang for the buck is an exciting challenge. If one day my rich Uncle Rocky Feller got out of the poorhouse and decided to slip $7,000 into my fake Chanel bag, maybe I would then go to the fancy curtain store and dole out the cash. But right now I need to make money stretch.

Spiritual

One Bible passage that challenges my tendency for vanity is found in Isaiah 55:2: "Why do you spend money for what is not bread, and your wages for what does not satisfy? Listen carefully to Me, and eat what is good, and let your soul delight itself in abundance" (NKJV). My husband, Emmitt, is very good at living out this verse and likes to gently remind me of its truth often. Thankfully, he is very kind in his response to the rolling of my eyes. Yet I'm glad to have his help in reminding me that ultimately my kinship is not to the Rockefellers but to the Rock of Ages.

Isn't it convicting to know that as Christians part of our stewardship is to not waste money on frivolous things? We're to spend the money God gives us wisely.

My husband and I make a concerted effort to live within our means, but it's not easy, especially when we're surrounded by offers of easy credit and told we "deserve" the best. How simple it would be for us to buy the car of our dreams. All we would have to do is stroll into a dealership and—voila!—within a matter of minutes we'd be driving a brand-new Lexus sedan (and make it bright red!). But the fact that we can't afford a Lexus without going into debt up to our eyeballs clues me into knowing it wouldn't be wise to make a purchase like that. We wouldn't be following our biblically rooted mandate to be "good stewards" of our resources. While we would be driving a fabulous car, our kids would have to eat seat leather. Yes, it is a challenge to live within our means, but it is worth every penny not spent to know we're doing what God wants us to do. The bottom line is that ultimately our money is not ours. It is God's. He's graciously fulfilled His promise to meet our needs.

The Deal Hunter

My dad is a big-time hunter. He lives and breathes the chase in the woods. Growing up I learned a lot about hunting—mainly that I wouldn't enjoy chasing and mortally maiming critters. But I also learned that there is a change in a man when he comes home with a kill. I remember my dad and brother coming home with big grins of victory on their faces when they "got one," but I also recall the many times I saw frowns of defeat when they came home empty-handed.

In my approach to finding chic in the cheap aisles, I'm like a hunter. A hunter of deals…and I rarely come home defeated.

The joy of victory when I find a great deal is intense. But like hunting, sometimes we have to do a little stalking to find the great discounts. I love shopping at thrift stores, junk stores, and antique stores. I have to dig around to find what I want, but the payoff can be huge. I once found a genuine Chanel scarf for six dollars at an antique store. That Chanel scarf was "mountable"! My dad was very proud of my kill.

Saving Money

Now that the *why* of saving money is done, let's get to the interesting and fun stuff. Let's address the *how*—what we can do to get the most value and quality for our bucks. My forte is decorating and entertaining, so I'll focus on how we can do both in a chic and cheap way.

Delicious and Memorable Dinner Parties

When my husband, Emmitt, and I were first starting out we lived in a small apartment. I loved throwing dinner parties even though our dining room was the size of a closet. Restricted by limited resources, I found a simple way to bring a big dazzle to our small surroundings while not spending a ton of money. The secret is to create a memorable table setting. While the food that is served can "make a statement" (we'll get to the food next), I put a lot of thought and effort into making the appearance of the table the center of attention. I discovered that if the table setting looked and felt welcoming, elegant, and memorable, the rest of the house (clean and presentable, of course) would feel more warm and inviting and spacious. And even more important than the hope of leaving the impression in our visitors' minds that our apartment was our personal palace, I found that a beautiful, well-planned table setting also makes the guests feel important and honored.

Even though we've now moved to a full-size home, I still see the dinner table and setting as the main way to set the mood, to make the party successful.

Everyone will gather and probably spend the bulk of the time at the table. So why not focus the decorating energy on that area? There are many ways to save money and still create a delightful atmosphere. Start with the appearance of the table. If it has a beautiful wood surface with no scratches or dents, save on the cost of a tablecloth by showing off the fine craftsmanship. Leave it uncovered. If the table isn't perfect, use a tablecloth. I keep a small assortment of inexpensive, simple-yet-elegant tablecloths. Neutral colors are more universally usable and are the best choice. No matter what color a dining room is, white or cream will always complement and add elegance. Damask prints are classy for fancy gatherings, and simple cotton cloths work well for less formal parties.

Now we can move to the creation of a centerpiece. Centerpieces can be many different styles, depending on your taste and the type of party you're hosting. A formal dinner party needs elegance and simplicity. The ideal for formal parties are white roses. To save money, fresh white carnations and inexpensive white votive candles can be just as elegant. When using fresh flowers, why not create the arrangement yourself, saving the cost of a florist's services? Keep the arrangement easy by using one kind of flower. Baby's breath or other greenery isn't necessary. In most cases, the simpler the color scheme, the more elegant the presentation.

A casual dinner party can be also be easy and nice. When the party is formal, I prepare the plates and arrange the food in the kitchen and take them to guests in the classic fashion. (Note: I do the serving to save money.) When I'm hosting a casual party I serve the food family style, which means all the food is brought to the table in bowls and on platters to be passed around by everyone. With family style you can save even more cash by foregoing the expense of a centerpiece, such as fresh flowers, and use a main dish food item as the table focus. When I serve Mexican food, I use a festive "South of the border" chips and salsa tray as the centerpiece.

On a more traditional note, a beautiful platter of meat, such as a tasty turkey, can also be a great focal point. In addition, it brings a certain homespun warmth to the table, like that found in Norman Rockwell paintings. Even better, using a main dish food item eliminates the need for buying fresh flowers or other decorative items. For a "down home" table, add a little sparkle through the dancing light given off by a pair of lit candles.

The next item to consider is place settings. Dishes come in such a wide variety of styles. I inherited my mother's affection for fine china, but also saw her practice thrift in purchasing. Though mom has five sets of china, none of them were purchased at retail price. She opted for the dishes that are "seconds"—ones with slight flaws so they're marked down in price. She carefully searched outlet malls for dishes that had flaws only on the underside. Her diligence in finding the best deals yielded dishes she's proud to own.

When I got married I was given a twelve-place setting of really nice china. With a money-saving head start like our wedding reception gave us, plus a few delightful dish discoveries on my own and with my hawkeyed mother in the aisles of some antique and thrift stores, I now have extra sets of dinnerware. (Yes, I'm working on my own collection.) One of my favorite sets was purchased by my groom *before* we got married. My thrifty husband found them on sale at a great price. (He knew the way to a woman's heart was through her dishes—smart man!) My other favorite set is my everyday china, which is the Johnson Brothers Old Britain Castles in pink. They are burgundy and white with castle scenes in the middle. My kitchen colors are burgundy, black, and gold, so the plates look great on my table and the cost wasn't at all extravagant. My other favorite set (can you see by now they are all favorites?) are my white dishes with pink flowers on them, which I use for spring/summer luncheons. I paid a whopping $30 for a set of eight at a discount home store.

I'm deeply grateful that my cabinets are filled with dishes suitable for various situations. But if your choices are more limited, I suggest white dishes. They are neutral and work well with formal and informal table settings. And better yet, they are easily replaced. So fret not if your dish shelves are currently bare—go for the simple white dishes. They'll serve you well and usually are very reasonable in price.

Let's move on to silver or flatware. There are nearly as many inexpensive options as there are tables to put them on. The choice you make depends on your taste. I found a very nice set of flatware at Target several years ago and still use them. The key question to ask isn't whether they are genuine silver or sterling silver. (After all, polishing is really not that much fun, is it?) Instead, check to make sure the flatware pieces are heavy enough and match. I recommend buying 18-gauge flatware because it feels solid and doesn't bend easily. With stemware, again the choice of styles is personal. Having a matched set adds to the table's classy look. With nice cloth napkins, nearly any set of flatware and stemware will look presentable.

Now the inexpensive-but-beautiful china is on the table, the candles found on sale are lit, the royalty free soft music from the local classical music radio station is playing in the background, and the guests are enjoying their visit. What could possibly contribute more joy to the evening? Good food!

The Food

When the food is really good, the "chic can be cheap" effort put into making the table look nice will be doubly enjoyed. Guests will go away with compliments on their lips if they are licking them. But beware, just like the temptation to overspend on dishes can tamper with the goal of economy, what is served at a party can break the bank if care is not given to making the menu budget friendly.

For the budget-minded person, hosting great dinner parties
is as much an attitude as anything else. Have fun while
getting the best bargains. Be creative and experiment.

Remember that my husband and I agreed on a monetary budget? It is not a policy that is abandoned when it comes to food. I'm sure you can relate. With only a certain amount of money to spend each month on groceries, we have to watch the amount spent on dinner parties. Fortunately there are some very tasty dishes that can be created with limited funds, and they can be special enough to be served even in a formal setting. One of my favorite recipes to make for company is my mother's "Spaghanza." It is lasagna made with spaghetti noodles. I always get rave reviews on the dish, and I especially enjoy sharing that it's my mother's recipe. It can feed a lot of folks for a little money. To help you save even more pennies by not having to invest in a phone call to my mother to get the recipe, here it is!

SPAGHANZA

Spaghetti
1 pound hamburger or ground turkey
1 large onion, chopped
1 jar prepared spaghetti sauce
1 16-oz. container cottage cheese
1 16-oz. container sour cream
Grated cheddar cheese

Prepare the spaghetti noodles as directed on the package.

Brown and drain the meat and onion. Add spaghetti sauce and let simmer.

In a separate bowl, combine cottage cheese and sour cream.

Spray a rectangular baking dish with vegetable spray. Put the cooked spaghetti in the bottom of the dish. Spread the cottage cheese/sour cream mixture on top of the spaghetti. Then spread on the meat sauce. Top with as much or as little grated cheddar cheese as desired. (You can do this in layers if you wish, I usually just do one layer to save time and energy.)

Bake for 60 minutes (or longer if needed) at 350 degrees until brown and bubbling.

Serve with salad and crusty bread.

Sometimes I take the money I save through thrift and invest in a little more extravagance for my visitors' taste buds. Going with the idea of keeping costs down, I've found that shopping at cooperative clubs such as Sam's Wholesale or Costco accomplishes the goal. One of my very favorite items to cook and serve is available there—and it invariably gets rave reviews. This salmon dish I got from my college roommate. Her father is a fabulous chef, and the following is his delicious creation.

SPECTACULAR SALMON

3 to 4 oz. salmon fillets (preferably fresh)
1 lime
2 tablespoons minced garlic
White cooking wine
Olive oil

Heat oven to 400 degrees.

Put salmon fillets in a deep baking dish side by side, skin side down. Squeeze fresh lime juice over each fillet. Add minced garlic, spreading it over each piece of meat. Pour olive oil and white wine over the salmon evenly until it covers the fillets.

Marinate in refrigerator for 30 minutes.

Bake at 400 degrees for 30 minutes or until the salmon is cooked through.

Serve with steamed asparagus and wild rice.

If I spend extra on the main course, I save money on the sides. A tasty salad and bread, for example, can be low cost and highlight an expensive main dish very nicely. If salad and bread are served, then appetizers aren't needed, which again saves money.

If appetizers are desired though, here are some economical yet tasty recipes.

BRUSCHETTA

1 French baguette
Mozzarella cheese
1 jar bruschetta topping

Heat oven to 350 degrees.

Cut bread into thin slices. Top each slice with a slice of mozzarella cheese and bake until cheese is melted and slightly browned.

Take out of oven and top each slice with a tablespoon of bruschetta.

Serve immediately.

HOT CRAB DIP

1 8-oz. block cream cheese
½ cup mayonnaise
1 can crab meat (drained)
¼ cup minced onion
1 teaspoon of lemon juice
⅛ teaspoon of hot pepper sauce

Combine and beat all ingredients until smooth.

Spoon into a small ovenproof dish sprayed with vegetable spray.

Bake at 350 degrees for 30 minutes, until it looks like it's browning on top.

Serve with crackers.

Everyone I've ever made this for has wanted more!

If you have company coming in late and you don't want to cook a lot, serve this dip with crackers, fresh cut vegetables, and a fruit plate. It's amazing how satisfying yet light this snack is.

For the budget-minded person, hosting great dinner parties is as much an attitude as anything else. Have fun while getting the best bargains. Be creative and experiment. You're only limited by your imagination (okay…and your budget).

Overnight Guests

One of my closest friends has the gift of hospitality. My husband and I took a trip to visit Sarah and her husband, Jonathan. We stayed overnight in their home, and when I woke up the next morning I was amazed at what I found. Outside our door was a beautiful silver tray with fresh, hot coffee and two cups on saucers. A small vase of flowers looked festive on the tray. I enjoyed every sip of java while I was getting ready for the day. When I went to the kitchen I found Sarah cooking a lovely breakfast. I told her I felt I was staying at the "Ritz Cantrell." That little act of hospitality blessed me immensely. The coffee wasn't expensive, but the presentation was exquisite. She didn't spend a lot of money, but she blessed this overnight guest. All it took was some effort and creativity.

Overnight guests represent a unique monetary challenge because it can cost more to pamper them than just hosting people at a dinner party. Yet with care and thought, the provisions needed for making overnighters feel special and comfortable don't have to be expensive.

For the most part, wallet-friendly comfort food, such as the Spaghanza dish mentioned earlier, is usually very well received.

For breakfast, on most mornings I serve "continental style," which is an assortment of cold cereals, muffins, yogurt, juice, and coffee. This can be a healthy beginning to the day. To add pizzazz, I fill a large bowl with ice and place cartons of yogurt in it. I place the muffins in a cloth-lined bread bowl. The orange juice goes in a beautiful glass pitcher. Affordable can be presentable.

Lunch, like a dinner party, can be done inexpensively yet be memorable. It's not the price of the food as much as the presentation. Be imaginative yet keep it simple.

The Guestroom

While in college my husband (my boyfriend at the time) invited me to visit his family in Atlanta for the weekend. I said yes, but I was very nervous. The drive from our college town to Atlanta seemed to last forever. When we arrived, I was greeted by his mother, Tish. To my pleasant surprise all my anxieties left me the moment we met at their front door. She offered such a warm welcome. Not only did she make me feel special, she made me feel like part of the family. When I was shown to my room, there was a wrapped gift on the bed with my name on it. I knew a guest should always bring the host a gift, but I'd never received a guest gift. I felt so cared for, prepared for, and honored.

Small, inexpensive touches can make
guests feel welcomed and loved.

Following Tish's very thoughtful example, ever since then I have gifts for overnight guests waiting for them in their room. This isn't anything pricey, just something small that shows I thought about them in advance of their arrival. A candle, beautiful notecards, a cup and saucer are nice gifts. Sometimes I give a welcome basket instead of a gift. The arrangement usually consists of a crunchy snack, a sweet snack, a small travel candle, and a large bottle of sparkling mineral water. In fact, I always have a large bottle of water with glasses on the nightstand, whether I'm doing a gift or a basket.

I also have chocolate on the nightstand or on their pillows. One thing I add to my guest room is a basket of magazines and books, along with a very cozy throw. I select magazines I know will interest my guests. For instance, if my friend Sarah is coming I have home decorating magazines available. She and her husband are building their dream home, and I know she will be interested in decor. Small, inexpensive touches can make guests feel welcomed and loved.

Another special touch for overnight visitors is having an assortment of toiletries and items, such as fresh towels, earmarked just for them in the bathroom they will use. Because I don't have a separate guest bathroom, I made it a point not to decorate our young daughter's bathroom with child-driven décor such as Elmo rugs, a Cinderella shower curtain, or Winnie the Pooh window treatments. Instead the bath is decorated in a lovely vintage theme (which our daughter will like later). Though the bathroom looks very classy, I didn't forsake my chic but cheap rule. On the wall are makeup ads dated 1954 that I cut out from an old magazine and framed. The shower curtain is a soft, pink-and-gold damask that I bought at a discount. The trash can is pink metal from the 1950s, and the counter has a small, fancy lamp that gives a soft glow that I found on sale. On the top of the toilet tank is a large basket filled with travel-sized toiletries. I included everything I could think of that a guest might need: shampoo and conditioner, body wash, lotion, toothbrushes, toothpaste, nail file, tissues, and a razor. Because hair care is particularly important to women, I splurged and got upscale shampoo and conditioner. Because they were travel size, I really didn't spend that much extra.

The Bottom Line

Cutting expenses when entertaining doesn't have to be drudgery. In fact, it can be easy and classy...if we're careful. My best advice is to follow the rule of SPEC when preparing for a dinner party or guests.

> **S**immplicity—From the dinner table to the guest room care basket, keep in mind that it doesn't take a plethora of items to make a guest feel honored. It's all in the...

> **P**resentation—The eyes of most guests, or even the more scrutinizing guests, are not really that hard to please. It's not what they see, but what they feel that sets the mood. To accomplish that goal, it takes just a little extra...

> **E**ffort—It's easy to spend money but it takes creative effort to save...

> **C**ash.

7

Showing Off or Showing You Care?

Doing something special for family or friends is a great way of expressing our love for them. However, one of the most important aspects of that act of generosity, whether it is in the form of gifts or service, is *knowing our audience.* Being cognizant of who we're dealing with and paying attention to their individual tastes are just as important and just as much a part of the present as the actual gift.

Let me (Annie) give a very personal example. My husband, Steve, knows me very well and has accepted the fact that I'm probably not the typical wife when it comes to giving gifts. On our thirtieth wedding anniversary Steve did the sensible thing and asked me what he could get me to celebrate our three decades of marital bliss. Okay, I realize I just said Steve knows me, so are you wondering, "Why does he need to ask you what you want for your anniversary?" Steve knows that I would rather he ask me my preference and give me the opportunity to say what I want than for him to guess. He knows I don't like to be surprised with something I don't want, doesn't fit, or can't use. (I know some women want to be surprised. If that's you, remember your spouse isn't a mind reader.)

On this special anniversary I asked for and received a beautiful, moderately expensive, perfectly fitting…Roto-Tiller. Yes, I tend to be rather practical. I needed something to help me plow up my extensive vegetable garden plot. Yep! That's what I wanted. Perhaps I shouldn't admit it, but I've also been guilty of asking for a treadmill for Valentine's Day and a vacuum cleaner for Christmas.

(Just in case there's a man reading this chapter, let me warn you that practical, functional gifts such as these may guarantee you a room at the local YMCA or at least a stint in the doghouse if your wife doesn't specifically ask for them. Consider her tastes and outlook when giving gifts.)

Couture or Casual?

Without question, it's important to know your spouse when gift giving. That same attitude carries over into hospitality. Unfortunately, I learned this truth the hard way. Some friends and I decided to give a wedding shower to a young woman who was marrying the son of one of our good friends. I agreed to hold the event at my house and was thrilled to have an excuse to break out all the finery and throw a shower party that would not soon be forgotten.

No expense was spared. The menu was elaborate, the decorations were beautiful, and the flowers were impressive. A couple of women took great pride in creating exquisite invitations replete with frills and feathers. (There really were feathers attached to the invitations.)

We started out wanting to be a blessing to our friend and her daughter-in-law-to-be. Our intentions were commendable.

Every detail was carefully attended to. The mode of dress was indicated on the invitation: "Casual elegance, Sunday best." The women and I worked ourselves into a frenzy. And everything was perfect. No doubt about it, it was our finest hour. As the guests arrived we were terribly impressed with ourselves. Every comment made added to our assurance that we had done a terrific job putting this shower together. I could hardly wait until the bride-to-be arrived and saw all that we'd done for her. We even had a lovely feather boa of feathers waiting to place around her shoulders, crowning her "the princess bride."

I was taken aback when the young lady and her mother arrived. To my surprise the bride-to-be was wearing a simple pair of corduroy pants and a plain sweater. Her mother was wearing a cotton jumper and a T-shirt.

In all our preparations for the evening, one critical detail was neglected. We failed to take into account who the party was for. The bride-to-be was not a feather boa gal. She was a jeans and sweatshirt woman.

We got our eyes off what was really important. We confused performance with hospitality. We were "showing off" instead of "showing we care."

A couple of the ladies who helped plan and execute the shower were disappointed in the young lady's lack of panache and commented that they thought the bride-to-be and her mother were rude for ignoring the dress code. But that wasn't true. After the party was over and I reflected on the happenings of the day, I realized that the rudeness on display that afternoon was not on the part of the young lady and her mother. No, it was placed squarely on the shoulders of those of us who did what *we* wanted to do, regardless of the taste and the individual style of our guest of honor. Never once did we ask her what she wanted. Never once did we ask how she felt about what we were doing.

We started out wanting to be a blessing to our friend and her daughter-in-law-to-be. Our intentions were commendable. But somewhere along the way we got our eyes off what was really important. We confused performance with hospitality. Unfortunately we were "showing off" instead of "showing we care."

Though I felt terribly bad about my errant attitude regarding the event, I didn't abandon my gift of hospitality. Instead, I thought it through and determined to not repeat the same mistake. That's when I remembered the often-told story about two women in the Bible who are forever linked to hospitality. "Is it showing off or showing love" is highlighted in Martha and Mary of Bethany. Their familiar story is in the book of Luke, chapter 10, verses 38-42.

> Now as they were traveling along [Jesus and His disciples, which may have included as few as 12, but perhaps as many as 70], He entered a village; and a woman named Martha welcomed Him into her home. She had a sister called Mary, who was seated at the Lord's feet, listening to His word. But Martha was distracted with all her preparations; and she came up to Him and said, "Lord, do You not care that my sister has left me to do all the serving alone? Then tell her to help me." But the Lord answered and said to her, "Martha, Martha, you are worried and bothered about so many things; but only one thing is necessary, for Mary has chosen the good part, which shall not be taken away from her."

Through the years I've heard this scripture used many times to excoriate those who tend to be "Martha types." In case you're wondering what or who this is, they are people who get a little self-consumed under the pressure of taking care of the many details required for being a host. Martha etched her reputation into history that day for having her focus in the wrong place when *the Guest* and His friends came to her house.

Because I find a certain camaraderie with Martha, let's look at a couple of facts about her situation that can be taken into account. First, the heart of generosity Martha showed by inviting such a large number of people into her home for meals and housing is extraordinary. If it were only 12 folks, it was still a sizable group. I don't know many women in my circle of friends who would be quick to take on providing for such a significant number of people, myself included. And what if there were 70 guests!

Second, there was a lot on the line for Martha. There were two ways a woman distinguished herself in that Middle Eastern society. She could either be the mother of many children or she could excel in hospitality. Since there is no mention of a husband or offspring,

Martha may have been single. This may be inferred by the fact that the house Martha invited Jesus and His fellow travelers to stay in was called "Martha's home."[1]

The bottom line is that having a houseful of guests is not a small undertaking for anyone, especially someone who may only have a small preparation team. The kitchen must have been a madhouse! How nice it would have been if Martha could have conveniently called for Chinese take-out or gone to the Bible-day equivalent of a KFC and bought a few buckets of chicken. In addition to the massive amount of food that would have been needed, there were other needs to tend to that were just as critical to the welfare of the guests.

When a person took on the responsibility for hosting a group of people in those days they also assumed the task of providing shelter and entertainment. As if that weren't enough, the host was also responsible to provide for any of the animals the guests may have brought along.[2] No wonder Martha was feeling a bit stressed by the commitment to host so many people and critters! Frankly, because the same thing happens to me when I take on more than I can handle, I have a heart of sympathy for Martha's riled reaction to being left with the whole load of work.

I imagine Jesus saying, "Martha, the food you are preparing smells great...The place looks wonderful...But the devil has gotten into your details. Your focus on the many things has caused you to turn inward and away from Me."

While I'm in no way justifying Martha's misplaced priorities pointed out in the passage, I do feel that her asking for help wasn't unreasonable. I would have likely done the same. And I don't believe for a minute that Jesus' reaction to her request for Him to compel Mary to lend a hand was meant to demean the work Martha was doing. Neither was His reprimand an indication that He wasn't grateful for the necessary provisions she was making. To the contrary, His statement, "You are worried and bothered about so many things," seems to reveal that He did take note of all the labor she was putting in to making His visit a success.

Martha's problem arose not when she asked for help, but when she verbalized her doubt that Christ cared about her. She'd convinced herself that if Jesus had any concern at all for her plight, He would have told Mary to lend a hand. Here's how I picture the scene at Martha's house that day Jesus talks to Martha:

> Martha, of course I care. But there's something I must point out to you. All you are doing is indeed important and believe Me, I do see it. You haven't stopped moving since I got here. The food you are preparing smells great, and I have no doubt it will satisfy us. The place looks wonderful, and I love what you've done with the windows. But Martha, the devil has gotten into your details. Your focus on the many things that are bothering you has caused you to turn inward and away from me. As a result, your concerns have become the center of your attention.

> If all you care about is your own agenda, then Martha, this visit is not about Me, it's about you. It might appear that Mary is being lazy and completely selfish, but you must understand that she has caught the aroma of another kind of bread. What I have to say while I'm here is manna from heaven and meant to nourish the heart. By choosing to sit and listen to me, Mary is offering another kind of service to me. It's not better than what you're doing, it's just that her service has eternal implications. Yours, while it's certainly needed, is temporary.

> You assumed that what I needed most as a guest was what you can do. But what I want more than anything is what you are. Mary has found the true heart of worship. By giving me her ears, she is giving her heart to me. And that is her way of showing she loves me. Please don't think I don't appreciate your hospitality, but why not take a break from it and let me

take care of you for a while by pouring something eternal
into the cup of your spirit.

Jesus' recorded words are as relevant today as the very air that you
and I are breathing this moment. He pointed out two important truths
to Martha—and to us all—to help us avoid the sad mistake of allowing
hospitality to become a show instead of a shower of blessing.

First, it's crucial that we know our audience. This is the first step in
knowing how to best serve them. Mary understood what Jesus desired
while at Martha's house were the ears on their heads, not just the ears
of corn on His plate, so to speak. Perhaps you will have guests in the
future who need your willingness to listen more than the fine table
you're so good at presenting. Or there might come a time when your
visitors need silence and rest instead of conversation. Finding out their
needs and putting them above your own pleases the heart of God and
your guests (see Philippians 2:2-4).

Second, the moment the focus turns from the needs of the guests
to fretting over the details of serving, the host ceases to be a servant
and steps up onto the performance stage. Martha learned that incred-
ibly important lesson. May God help us to glean from it as well so
that we don't waste our time doing a song and dance that never gets
His applause.

8

Feeding Family and Friends

For some of us there is no greater challenge than to stand up and deliver a speech to a crowd, regardless of how many people are in attendance. Our hearts begin to race, our breathing becomes labored, and our sweat glands go into overtime. It's not a pleasant experience, to say the least. Just as difficult as it may be for some to give a public oratory, the same terror-filled emotions can also grip some people when asked to entertain, no matter how many people may be involved. I asked several women to share their greatest dread when it comes to offering hospitality:

- I'm disorganized. It's hard for me to get all the work done that needs to be done.

- I'm not a good cook, and I don't like to do it.

- It's hard for me to entertain and not spend more money than I should.

- I want everything to be perfect, and I'm not happy if it isn't. I've found it easier to not do it at all if I can't do it the way it should be done.

- I'm not a very good housekeeper, so when I have company coming, getting my house ready is a big job and a big deal.

- I'd love to invite people over, but we have so little space. It's hard to fit extra people in when we're already crowded.

- Being the mother of small children, I hesitate having people in my home because we have so many toys. It's hard to keep things nice.

- My house is so filled with clutter and stuff, entertaining seems out of the question. Before I can invite others into my house I need to get rid of a bunch of stuff.

- I like to invite people over to our house, but my husband is such a control freak and perfectionist. He worries if things aren't perfect. It's easier to not have anyone come over than to listen to him criticize and complain.

- My husband and I have two huge, overly friendly dogs. I'd love to have folks come to my house, but my dogs keep me from inviting them. Not only are the dogs intimidating and rather intrusive, but they also shed a lot. I'm afraid for people to sit down. I know they're going to be covered with dog hair when they get up.

- I have very high expectations of myself when it comes to entertaining. I want everything prepared and ready before my guests arrive. Sometimes I wear myself out before they ever arrive because of all the cleaning and cooking involved.

- I don't like to have people over because I'm afraid they will judge me and my husband. Our house is not as nice as some of our friends' homes.

- I know I should be more hospitable, but seriously, I just don't have the time it takes to get ready for company. It's just easier to not do it.

From feeling disorganized to lacking an entertainment budget, the reasons for hesitating to have guests in a home are varied. Each one merits attention, but there's another response many women shared:

> I need help knowing what to serve to my guests. I want
> to entertain, but I need some good ideas for menus and

refreshments. Now that our children are grown and gone, I rarely cook anymore so I'm out of practice and out of ideas.

Becoming an "empty nester" can certainly result in feeling out of practice. What are other issues that interfere? Careers that feed on massive amounts of time and energy can consume a person's presence in the kitchen. One lady said, "I've noticed that as I've become better at being a nurse, I've become worse as a cook."

We don't have to be Rachael Ray, Paula Deen, or Martha Stewart to entertain and make our guests feel special.

For many of us it is quite easy to fall out of practice. We begin to feel intimidated by the idea of having guests. But this book will help! We're going to offer you some menus and recipes that can help alleviate apprehension and boost confidence.

Many of the women I spoke to had unrealistic expectations of what was necessary to take care of and feed guests. Most thought they had to have a wide range of recipes. However, if you stop and think about it, the majority of us have about seven different things we cook most of the time. I have a kitchen cabinet full of cookbooks and yet, when it comes down to it, I basically serve the same things day after day. It's fun to try new menus and recipes, but we don't have to be as innovative as we might think. The following recipes are tasty and easy to make. We don't have to be a Rachael Ray, Paula Deen, or Martha Stewart to entertain and make our guests feel special.

These effort-friendly, guest-pleasing, quick-and-easy recipes provide main meal provisions of protein, vegetables, and bread. Some will satisfy the desire for something sweet that most guests have. Each recipe has been table-tested through the years by my family and friends. Others have been submitted by friends who also love entertaining and giving hospitality.

BREAKFAST MENU
Breakfast Casserole

Mixed Fresh Fruit

Banana Bread

Frozen hash brown potatoes

1 pound sausage

12 eggs

½ cup milk

Salt

Pepper

Cheddar cheese

Pour frozen hash brown potatoes in the bottom of a rectangular baking dish.

Brown sausage and drain on a paper towel. Place sausage on top of hash browns.

Crack eggs into a bowl. Whip with milk and season with salt and pepper. Pour egg mixture on top of sausage.

Grate as much cheddar cheese on top as you desire.

Cover and chill overnight.

Bake at 325 degrees uncovered for an hour. Tent with foil if it starts to brown too soon.

Feeds 6 to 8, depending on appetites.

Add toast or English muffins for a very nice and easy breakfast.

BANANA BREAD

½ cup vegetable oil
1 cup honey
2 eggs, beaten
3 bananas (ripe and smashed)
2 cups self-rising flour
1 teaspoon baking soda
3 tablespoons milk
½ teaspoon vanilla extract
½ to 1 cup chopped nuts

Beat honey and oil together.

Add eggs and bananas and beat well.

Add flour and baking soda, milk, and vanilla and stir. Add nuts and stir.

Pour into muffin or bread pan. Bake at 350 degrees until solid and brown. For bread loaf it takes at least an hour, depending on your oven.

MENU

Breakfast Burritos

Hash Brown Potatoes

Cheese Grits

Fresh Fruit or Melon

BREAKFAST BURRITOS

1 pound sausage

1 dozen eggs

¼ cup milk or cream

Salt

Pepper

½ stick butter

Cheddar cheese, grated

Whole-wheat tortillas

Optional

Green peppers

Onions

Brown sausage in a skillet. Drain on paper towels and set aside.

Using the same skillet, beat eggs, adding milk or cream and salt and pepper to taste.

Melt butter in separate skillet. Pour in egg mixture and scramble as they cook.

Using a flat griddle or separate skillet sprayed with vegetable spray, warm a tortilla thoroughly on both sides. Place on a paper towel-covered plate. Keep adding tortillas, separating each one with paper towels.

Take each tortilla and place scrambled eggs, cooked sausage, and grated cheese in the middle. Roll up like a burrito.

I made these one day when my daughter, Heidi, and her husband, Emmitt, were moving. I wrapped each one in aluminum foil. During the move the willing helpers could grab a breakfast burrito and chow down. It was compact, convenient, and yummy.

Hint: You can serve jelly, salsa, or honey with the burritos. This is also something you can make early and reheat when it's time to eat.

MENU
Sausage Rolls

Eggs

Old-fashioned Oatmeal

Stephanie's Favorite Rosemary Potatoes

SAUSAGE ROLLS

Biscuit dough or canned biscuits
Flour
1 pound sausage, thawed

Make biscuit dough or use canned biscuits.

Roll the biscuits out on an amply floured surface to about ½ inch thick. Take 1 pound of raw sausage and evenly disperse it over the biscuit dough.

With plenty of flour on hand, roll the biscuit dough and sausage into a long tubular shape. Continually flour the counter so the biscuit dough won't stick to the surface or your hands. Continue to roll dough until it can be cut into cinnamon roll-like pieces. Place the "sausage dough" on a slightly greased cookie sheet with the raw sausage visible.

Bake for 20 to 30 minutes at 350 degrees or until sausage is well cooked.

This is what my son always wanted for his birthday breakfast during his growing up years. Your guests are bound to rave over this yummy dish.

OLD-FASHIONED OATMEAL

Prepare according to package instructions. Serve with brown sugar, dried cranberries, bananas, walnuts, raisins, and fruit (canned or fresh).

Hint: I like to offer healthy choices at meals, especially when the main course is great on taste but may be calorie laden. So when I fix something that is rather fattening and a special splurge, I always add something healthy, such as oatmeal, so my guests will feel free to choose what they want to eat.

STEPHANIE'S FAVORITE ROSEMARY POTATOES

Potatoes
Olive oil
Salt
Pepper
Rosemary, fresh or dried
Garlic powder

Cut up and quarter as many potatoes as you want. If you use red potatoes, you don't need to peel them. Just make sure they are clean and the eyes are cut out. I precook the potatoes in water to hurry up the baking time.

Toss the potato wedges in olive oil.

Salt and pepper to taste.

Sprinkle on fresh rosemary if you have it or you can use dried. Add a little garlic powder if you wish.

Place in a 350- to 400-degree oven. Bake uncovered for 1 hour.

My family loves this, so I always make a big cookie sheet of them.

LUNCHEON MENU 1
Chicken Casserole
Jeannie's Broccoli Salad
Green Beans
Chocolate Cheesecake Delight

CHICKEN CASSEROLE

3 chicken breasts or precooked chicken
16 oz. sour cream
1 can cream of mushroom soup
1 cup milk
1 package herb stuffing mix

Cook and bone a chicken, use three chicken breasts, or use a pre-cooked chicken.

Shred the chicken or cut into pieces.

Mix chicken, sour cream, soup, and milk.

Pour into a greased casserole dish.

Prepare stuffing per package instructions. Spoon over chicken mixture.

Bake at 350 degrees until heated through and lightly toasted on top, approximately 30 minutes.

This is a great dish for company because you can prepare it the day before. Make sure you refrigerate it. This dish provides the meat and the starch/bread for your meal.

JEANNIE'S BROCCOLI SALAD

My friend Jeannie Duncan shared this recipe with me many, many years ago. I've been making it ever since.

1 large head of broccoli (flowerets only)
4 oz. shredded Swiss cheese
12 slices of bacon, fried crispy
½ cup light mayonnaise
¼ cup sugar
1 tablespoon vinegar
2 tablespoons minced garlic

Mix the last four ingredients to make the dressing.

In a separate bowl, combine the broccoli flowerets, bacon, and cheese. Add the dressing, toss, and chill.

GREEN BEANS

Using a Crock-Pot and slowly cooking the beans gives them great flavor.

Green beans, frozen
Bacon or ham pieces
Salt
Pepper
Almonds, toasted (optional)

Place frozen green beans, along with bacon or ham pieces, in the slow cooker. Salt and pepper to taste and let them cook for several hours on low. Since beans are frozen, don't add water.

Add toasted almonds on top of green beans just before serving to add a little crunch.

CHOCOLATE CHEESECAKE DELIGHT

3 packages reduced-fat cream cheese, softened
3 eggs
½ cup sugar
1 teaspoon vanilla
1¾ cups (10 oz.) mini semi-sweet chocolate chips
1 graham cracker pie crust

Beat cream cheese and sugar in large bowl.

Add eggs and vanilla and beat well.

Stir in chocolate chips.

Pour into pie crust.

Bake for 10 minutes at 450 degrees. Do not open the oven door,
but turn temperature down to 250 degrees and cook an additional
30 minutes. Keep an eye on it. When it looks set, remove from the
oven and allow to cool on a wire rack.

Cover and refrigerate.

LUNCHEON MENU 2

Pita Sandwiches

Chips

Carrot, Celery, and Cucumbers with Ranch Dip

"Can't Go Wrong" Peach Cobbler

PITA SANDWICHES

2 large cans chicken breast meat
½ to 1 cup light mayonnaise
1 cup shredded cheese
1 cup red or white seedless grapes
½ cup chopped walnuts or pecans
Pita bread
Tomatoes
Alfalfa sprouts

Mix first 5 ingredients. Fill pita bread with meat mixture.

Top with chopped tomatoes and alfalfa sprouts.

"CAN'T GO WRONG" PEACH COBBLER

1 stick butter
1 cup sugar
1 cup self-rising flour
1 cup milk
1 large can of peaches, drained
Vanilla ice cream (optional)

Melt butter and pour into a loaf pan.

Combine the rest of ingredients (except ice cream) loosely. It's okay if there are lumps.

Pour into the loaf pan.

Bake at 350 degrees for 40 minutes, making sure the center is done.

The butter will come up around the edges and create a yummy buttery crust.

Serve alone or with a scoop of creamy vanilla ice cream.

Since the rest of the lunch is light and healthy, it's all right to splurge on dessert.

_____

DINNER MENU 1
Spaghanza

Spring Salad

Green Peas

Rolls

Waistline Friendly Key Lime Pie

SPAGHANZA

This is my special concoction. Although it has a strange name, it is always a winner when served to my family and friends. Heidi shared the recipe in chapter 6, page 63.

SPRING SALAD

1 bag spring lettuce
1 can mandarin oranges
1 apple, chopped
1 handful dried cranberries
Toasted almonds or hulled sunflower seeds
Raspberry and walnut vinaigrette dressing

Combine all ingredients except vinaigrette. Refrigerate.

Just before serving, toss with raspberry and walnut vinaigrette dressing.

This has become a real staple in our family meals. With the combination of nuts, fruits, and vegetables it is a meal in itself.

If you want, add grilled chicken or shrimp and you've got a fancier meal.

WAISTLINE FRIENDLY KEY LIME PIE

1 can fat-free, sweetened condensed milk
1 package (8 oz.) light cream cheese
⅓ cup key lime juice (or lemon juice)
1½ teaspoons vanilla
Graham cracker pie crust
Light whipped topping

Combine all ingredients (except crust) and beat until smooth.

Pour into graham cracker pie crust and chill until firm.

Top with light whipped topping.

DINNER MENU 2
Easy Elk Stroganoff
Layered Salad
Everything Fruit Dessert

EASY ELK STROGANOFF

Egg noodles
1 pound elk, venison, buffalo, or beef cut into strips
1 large onion, chopped
1 can cream of mushroom soup
8 oz. milk or water
Worcestershire sauce
8 oz. sour cream

Prepare noodles according to package instructions.

Crumble meat into skillet and add chopped onion.

Brown and drain, removing as much grease as possible. Add cream of mushroom soup and milk or water. Add a generous splash of Worcestershire sauce. After heating thoroughly, add sour cream. Do not boil.

Serve over the cooked noodles.

Some folks don't like venison or elk because they think it has a strong or wild taste. I've never had anyone refuse to eat this dish. The added ingredients temper any "wildness" the meat might have.

If you're more of a Daniel Webster than a Daniel Boone, ground chicken or turkey can be substituted for the meat.

LAYERED SALAD

Lettuce, shredded
Carrots, grated
Celery, chopped
1 cup mayonnaise
Green peas, cooked and drained
3 to 4 eggs, boiled and chopped
1 pound bacon, cooked and crumbled into bits
Cheese, grated

In a glass bowl, layer the ingredients in the order listed, ending with the grated cheese on top.

Chill and keep refrigerated until ready to serve.

This is an ageless recipe that is a staple at many church dinners. It's a great and beautiful way to serve vegetables.

EVERYTHING FRUIT DESSERT

2 cans mandarin oranges
1 20-oz. can pineapple chunks, drained
1 small package vanilla instant pudding, dry
½ cup shredded coconut
1 cup colored miniature marshmallows
1 cup juice (from the pineapple chunks)
2 to 3 bananas, sliced or chopped
Whipped topping
Pecans or English walnuts, chopped

Combine first 6 ingredients and pour into serving dish. Refrigerate at least 20 minutes.

Before serving add a layer of sliced bananas on top. Cover with whipped topping and sprinkle nuts on top.

DINNER MENU 3
Baked Chicken
Corn Casserole
Spring Salad
Fresh Fruit Salad

BAKED CHICKEN

You can make this as complicated or as simple as you wish.

Chicken
Flour (all-purpose)
Salt
Pepper
Butter or sauces (optional)

Wash and pat dry chicken. Remove skin and visible fat if desired or bake with the skin on for added moisture and flavor.

Coat chicken with all-purpose flour and salt and pepper to taste. Coat a cookie sheet with vegetable oil spray and place chicken on sheet. Spray chicken with vegetable oil. Add butter or other sauce if desired to add more flavor.

Bake at 375 degrees for 45 minutes or until juices run clear. Make sure chicken is cooked thoroughly.

CORN CASSEROLE

4 large eggs
$^2/_3$ cup safflower oil
1 teaspoon garlic salt
1 small box muffin mix
2 cans (1 lb. 10 oz. each) cream style corn
½ cup cheddar cheese, grated

Preheat oven to 375 degrees.

Crack eggs into a large bowl and beat well. Add oil and garlic salt. Mix well.

Stir in the dry muffin mix and cream corn until well blended.

Pour into greased baking pan. Sprinkle grated cheese on top.

Bake at 375 degrees for 50 to 60 minutes or until brown and puffed on top and the sides slightly pulled away.

Remove from oven and let set 5 to 10 minutes.

Great served hot or at room temperature.

SPRING SALAD

See "Dinner Menu 1" (page 93) for recipe. Feel free to add sunflower seeds, dried cherries, or other ingredients for taste variation.

FRESH FRUIT SALAD

Apples
Bananas
Grapes
Peaches, fresh or canned
Oranges or mandarin oranges (canned)
Strawberries, fresh or frozen
Coconut, toasted and shredded (optional)

Cut and mix fruit in large bowl. If using canned fruit, drain before adding. If you prefer, right before serving sprinkle toasted, shredded coconut on top.

Any fruit you enjoy will be great. You can't go wrong so be creative and even daring.

DINNER MENU 4
Hazel's Terrific Chicken Enchiladas

Mexican Layered Dip and Chips

Spanish Rice

Fruity Frozen Dessert

HAZEL'S TERRIFIC CHICKEN ENCHILADAS

3 chicken breasts or large can of chicken

1 can cream of mushroom soup

1 can cream of chicken soup

1 can Rotel Tomato Sauce with green chilis

1 can evaporated milk

2 cans enchilada sauce

Tortilla chips, broken

2 cups cheese, grated

Cook chicken and pull meat apart.

Mix chicken, soups, Rotel Tomato Sauce, and milk.

In a large casserole dish, alternate layers of chicken mixture, broken tortilla chips, and cheese. The last layer should be the cheese.

Bake at 400 degrees for about an hour until brown and bubbly.

MEXICAN LAYERED DIP AND CHIPS

16 oz. refried beans
1 package taco mix
1 cup sour cream
1 cup of guacamole, refrigerated
1 cup Mexican cheese, shredded
1 cup thick salsa
4 oz. can sliced green chilis
Green onions
Tortilla chips

Mix refried beans and taco mix in a small bowl. Spread in an 8-inch square dish.

Layer sour cream, guacamole, cheese, salsa, chilis, and green onions.

Bake at 350 degrees until heated all the way through or you can serve it cold.

Serve with tortilla chips.

SPANISH RICE

Prepare according to package instructions.

FRUITY FROZEN DESSERT

1 can condensed milk
8 oz. whipped topping
1 can cherry pie filling
1 small can of coconut
1 small can of crushed pineapple, well drained

Mix ingredients well and freeze.

More Great Choices

The following recipes are my favorites when entertaining a large number of people or just a few. These recipes come from my family or out of my own tomato-sauce-splattered, pages-falling-out recipe book. They were table-tested and approved by my family and friends.

All those who knew my mom quickly share that she was an incredible cook. She was known for several gastronomic jubilees, including her cherry pies (the recipe is a carefully guarded secret). Every potluck dinner, family reunion, and holiday celebration included Sylvia Williamson's mouth-watering masterpieces. One favorite delicacy my mom was also known for was her wonderful biscuits. We affectionately referred to them as "Sylvie biscuits." I've tried my hand at mastering this feat, and my family assures me I've succeeded. However, this past summer while visiting my sister, my family and I experienced a delicious culinary delight. Not only did Alice make "Sylvie biscuits," but they were better than mom's! Alice graciously gave me permission to include her recipe in this book.

SYLVIE BISCUITS

2 cups self-rising flour*
½ cup butter
1 cup milk or buttermilk
Flour
Crisco shortening

From Alice...

My husband, Karl, thought it was funny when I explained how to make my special biscuits. It's hard to give a recipe for something you just do, but here it is. Mix flour, butter, and milk together. Now, you have to put enough milk in them, but not too much. Work the dough, but not too long.

I use canola oil and bake the biscuits in a square glass baking dish. I think this really makes a difference in how they turn out.

Preheat the glass dish. This is the key to getting the biscuits to rise quickly. Since Mom would preheat her biscuit pan with a scoop of Crisco melting in it, that's what I do. She would take the biscuit dough that had been cut into large round shapes (if you don't have a biscuit cutter you can use the top of a glass dipped in flour) and flop each biscuit individually into the hot grease on each side. This would cause the biscuits to have a browned, crunchy bottom. Mom loved to take the bottom of the biscuit and dip it into her coffee. I can see her doing it as I write this. She always made everything look so yummy.

I bake them just like I would a cake: 350 degrees—at least in my oven. Yours may need to be 400 degrees.

---

* If you don't have self-rising flour on hand, make your own: Mix 4 cups all-purpose flour, 2 teaspoons salt, and 2 teaspoons baking powder. Store in a tightly covered container.

Specific Instructions

Combine self-rising flour with the butter and milk. Stir using a fork until the dough leaves the side of the bowl.

Put dough on a floured board. Knead gently and quickly, just until smooth.

Roll out to 1-inch thickness. Cut into biscuit shape with floured cutter or cup.

Place the biscuits close together in the glass pan if you want them to rise tall.

Bake at 350 to 400 degrees for 20 minutes or until as brown as you like them.

BECKY'S CHICKEN MARSALA

My sister Becky makes a delicious main course. She graciously agreed to share it. She said, "This is the best-tasting recipe I cook, and the one that gets the most rave reviews. I hope you enjoy it!"

1 pound of chicken strips
½ cup all-purpose flour
1 teaspoon salt
1 teaspoon pepper
Canola oil
1 cup chicken broth
1 cup Marsala wine
1 cup sliced mushrooms
Egg noodles or rice

Place chicken strips in a Baggie with flour, salt, and pepper. Coat thoroughly and pan fry them in canola oil. Drain oil and pat chicken dry with paper towels. Put back in skillet and add chicken broth, Marsala wine, and mushrooms. Simmer until mixture thickens.

Transfer to a baking dish and keep warm until ready to serve.

Prepare noodles or rice according to package instructions.

Serve chicken mixture over noodles or rice.

A good side dish is a vegetable medley from the frozen food section of the grocery store. It adds a nice color combination to the plate presentation.

QUICK AND EASY PUNCH

2 packages lemon-lime powdered drink mix
46 oz. can pineapple juice
1 cup sugar
2 quarts water
1 quart ginger ale

Mix all ingredients and chill.

Hint: Get extra pineapple juice or ginger ale and freeze to use as ice cubes. This way the taste isn't diluted as the ice melts. Be careful when freezing carbonated (or other) liquids. The contents may explode! To avoid this danger, transfer the ginger ale or pineapple juice into a container that has room for liquid expansion and is easy to get the ice out of.

OLD VIRGINIA WASSAIL

2 quarts sweet apple cider
2 cups orange juice
12 oz. frozen lemonade
46 oz. can pineapple juice
3 to 4 sticks whole cinnamon
2 tablespoons whole cloves
1½ cups sugar

Combine ingredients in pan. Simmer and strain into serving bowl.

Your guests will want this recipe!

SPINACH DIP

1 package frozen chopped or leaf spinach
1 can water chestnuts, chopped
1 package dry vegetable soup mix
1 cup light sour cream
1 cup light mayonnaise
1/3 cup green onions, chopped

Thaw the spinach and squeeze the water out. I use a colander and paper towels. It can be a mess, but get as much liquid out as possible.

Mix all ingredients together and chill.

Serve with chips or crackers.

Large Informal Party Menu

Don't let wondering what to serve keep you from the blessing of giving hospitality! This is a great menu for a large crowd for any occasion.

Prepare three kinds of soup and two kinds of sandwiches. Pair this great combo with some chips, fresh-cut veggies, cheese tray, and crab or spinach dip and crackers. I've served this to as many as 60 people. It's fun, inexpensive, and very tummy filling.

9

Reaching In

One of the most poignant quips I've heard about hospitality is: "Remember to treat company like family, and treat family like company." This statement is packed tight with wisdom, but it's not necessarily an easy attitude to adopt and follow. Still, my parents were worthy examples of how it worked to the benefit of kith and kin.

Growing up in a small community and being part of a large family was a combination that guaranteed hospitality was constantly in full-throttle at our house. With eight of us in the home and each one having our friends, fellow students, Sunday school classmates, coworkers, business associates, neighbors, and out-of-town acquaintances there was a steady flow of visitors. We even had a knack for bringing home strangers...as well as those who were just plain strange. There were always people coming and leaving. It was not uncommon for mom to have no idea of who and how many nonfamily members would be sitting at our supper table.

I commend my parents for their display of graciousness in the face of all the extra effort and expense it required to host all those invited in by my siblings and me. But what amazes me more than how willing they were to entertain "outsiders" on their tight budget, is how my folks managed to come up with the extra focus and funds needed to recognize each of their children's important milestones. Birthdays, sport victory parties, and graduations were wonderful times that made each of us know we were loved and a priority.

There is a great reward for doing things outside the home, such as hosting a dinner party at a senior center, taking a potluck dish for the Sunday school cookout, buying a sandwich for a homeless person on the street, helping throw a bridal shower for a young woman at church, and serving tea and cookies to a next-door neighbor. But the hazard that accompanies the very legitimate "reach out" commitment is that we can forget to "reach in." And, unfortunately, the people who often pay the price for outreach are the kids.

Who could possibly be more important recipients of a mother's gift of hospitality and entertaining than her own children? And the opportunities to bless them are endless. Like many of you, I've hosted numerous birthday parties for my kiddos during their growing-up years. We've been command central for countless sleepovers where our rafters rang with myriad voices of teenage girls talking endlessly about "who is going with whom." Our outdoor grill has been the temporary home for plenty of pounds of hamburger and chicken wings as our son and his friends fed their bodies and souls.

While it's impossible to detail all we did for our kids—and all you've done for yours—I'd like to highlight a special celebration in our family. Maybe this seed of an idea will take root in your heart... and bless your family! Our kids still talk about their individual experiences from each of their special celebrations and how much they knew (and know!) they are loved. Trust me—the effort and expense will be well worth it!

The Dedication Party

After each of our kids turned 12 we started planning a special event for them. The model for the evening can loosely be compared to the Jewish celebration of Bar and Bat Mitzvahs. We wanted to bring special attention and emphasis to the "coming of age" of each child, when Nathan and Heidi turned 13 and stepped from childhood into early adulthood.

Steve and I invited the people who were positive influences in our children's lives up until that time. Well in advance of the planned evenings we sent out the invitations for these special nights. The hand-written invitations included an encouragement to each guest to be prepared to verbally (and briefly) inspire and instruct the child being honored.

———

As they each held their "Book of Letters" in their hands
and leafed through them, the looks on their faces showed
they were very aware of how much planning and love
it took to create such an outpouring of support.

———

We also included a request to some of the guests asking them to write a letter to the child being honored for a memory book. Family, friends, and other special folks who loved them through the years and were profound influences on them willingly responded. Several who wrote the letters expressed how grateful they were to be asked to contribute to the collection and that they were given sufficient time to think through what they wanted to write. After receiving the letters we carefully placed them in a leather-bound book that could be zipped closed to protect the contents.

As parents we were humbled and extremely pleased when friends and family not only expressed appreciation for the purpose of our idea, but planned to fly in from out of state or drive the many hours it would take to attend. Many dear friends who lived close by made the effort to come and share in the celebration as well.

The event featured a lot of good food, gifts, and reconnecting with those who cared enough about our children to contribute to their lives through words and deeds. Three special moments became the highlights of each dedication.

The first special happening was when we formally presented the child of the hour with his or her "Book of Letters." As they held them in their hands and leafed through them on their nights, the looks on their faces showed they were very much aware of how much planning and love it took to create such an outpouring of support. Steve and I quietly agreed that we had helped create heirlooms Nathan and Heidi would treasure for a long time.

After we ate a delicious and festive meal, everyone gathered in the den for the second presentation. We placed the guest of honor in the center of the room on a chair. Encircled by family and friends, each listened as uplifting words and wisdom were shared. Steve and I were pleased and amazed at the thought and time the contributors obviously put into their comments. There were moments of laughter and times of tears as inspiring insights and lessons that would build up and help our children were shared.

The third special gift turned out to be the most important part of the evening. We had wonderful men of God (with Nathan) and lovely women of God (with Heidi) lay hands on them and pray prayers of dedication to the Lord's service. We recorded the prayers so through the years Nathan and Heidi could go back and remember how many people cared for them and that the decisions they make throughout life affect them—and those who have a vested interest in them.

These people continue to be an inspiration to our children, although they're adults now. When Nathan was 20 years old he was preparing to leave the United States to spend the summer in France. We asked the men of God who had been at his dedication celebration to come to the house to pray over him again. Nathan gave them permission to ask him any questions they wished upon his return. They were to keep him accountable in his commitment to prayer and his attendance to studying the Scriptures. They were also given permission to ask him questions about his commitment to living a godly, moral life. During that summer's stay in France, Nathan met his future wife, Stephanie. None of us could have known what a monumental summer it was going to be! Looking back on that time, I'm so grateful his trip was bathed in prayer, and he willingly chose to be held accountable by the honorable men who took part in his life for so many years.

If our children are a message we are sending to
a time that you and I will never see
Parents, let us all consider what we're writing on
their hearts for the generations to read

Since the dedication parties, our children have mentioned on more than one occasion how meaningful and memorable their events were. Of all the ways we "reached in" to our kids, this celebration stands out as the most unforgettable and meaningful. The insights and wisdom will hopefully last their lifetimes.

During the season of Nathan's dedication party Steve wrote the following lyric. Though it is his prayer, it vividly expresses the primary reason we chose to cover our children with words of spiritual encouragement and fervent prayers for their ongoing commitment to good morals and character. Maybe these words will inspire you to begin even now to reach in to your kids with this special gift of hospitality.

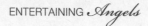
EVERYONE WITHIN ME

Bless the LORD, *O my soul,*
and all that is within me,
bless His Holy Name.

PSALM 103:1

If our children are a message we are sending to a time
that you and I will never see
parents, let us all consider what we're writing on their hearts
for the generations to read

As a father I am praying they will hear
that a man will be brave if Jehovah is his fear
and there's a strength in his weakness
when it's yielded to the Lord
and for a man there's cleansing in his tears

And may all that is within me
who are my flesh but are yet to be born
find these words I am writing on the wall of their hearts
blessed be the name of the Lord
let everyone within me bless the Lord

And with their mother I am praying
they will hear about the Bread
that will satisfy the hunger in their souls
and may they hear of Living Water so
they'll never thirst again
and may the Father's Son warm them when they're cold

And we are praying they will hear
about the wealth one can find
not in what we have but what we give away
and that there is no softer pillow
than a conscience that is clear
when we come to the end of the day[1]

10

Reaching Out

*Treat a man as he appears and you make him worse. But treat a man
as if he already were what he potentially could be,
and you make him what he could be.*

GOETHE

When we are open to opportunities that call us to be hospitable,
there are times when we are led into situations that make us feel
uncomfortable and require us to look past our predictable lives and
reach out into the lives of those who are hurting. In a survey I asked
women from various parts of the country the following question to see
how far outside "the box" some were willing to go to be hospitable.

*What would your response be if you were asked to give a baby
shower for a girl who is pregnant and not married?*

- I would say yes. It is a great way to show God's love to someone
  who really needs it.

- I would do it if I were close to the girl or her family.

- I would probably do it, but with a degree of caution about
  younger girls getting the wrong message. Even with my reservations, I believe all life is a gift from God, and the young
  girl in this situation needs love and support.

- I would consider this a great opportunity to minister to this
  young girl and her family. The Bible says that the world will

know we are Christ's disciples, not because we are right all the time, but because we have such extravagant love for one another.

- I was the young girl who was pregnant and unmarried. I felt shame and guilt. The situation was humiliating to me and I'm sure for my family as well. Those who showed me mercy were a lifeline at a vulnerable time in my life. I'll never forget them.

- I was an unmarried and pregnant teenager. I remember my family giving a baby shower for me and showing me great kindness in my difficult situation. A lot of those memorable feelings came back to me when I was recently invited to a baby shower for an expectant, unmarried girl in our very conservative church. Some of the women in our church judged and talked, while others reached out with love and gifts. I know we who were supportive made a positive difference, especially for the grandmother-to-be. I think the situation was very hard on her. She needed our friendship more than the girl needed our gifts.

- Our church had a young girl in this situation. We rallied around her, gave her a shower, and then the church adopted her and her child as part of our family. Isn't it when His people show love and forgiveness that we see the hands and heart of God at work?

- I am giving a baby shower for my daughter's friend who is in this situation. Do I worry that my daughter will get the wrong idea if I'm loving and accepting of this young girl? That perhaps she'll make the same bad decision her friend made? No. My daughter sees the pain and sacrifices being demanded of this girl. Seeing her friend go through all this is probably the most effective birth control or teaching on abstinence that my daughter could ever acquire.

- I would be honored to do so. So many times we condemn people for the wrongs they have done and fail to lend a helping hand. I was the young woman you speak of. I was raised in church and I knew I was wrong, but I hoped the church would offer a refuge. It would have been easier to have an abortion than to face the condemning eyes at church, but I couldn't do it. The ladies wanted to give me a baby shower, but I overheard the pastor's wife saying, "If we do this it's like we condone what she has done." I thank God some ladies found it in their hearts to help me. I did stay in church, and my son was raised in church. He is a fantastic musician in a wonderful church today.

- Of course I'd be glad to give a shower for a young girl in that situation. Of all the young girls having babies in our church, this girl who is all alone needs our help, support, and gifts.

- We had a young girl who went to our church "get in trouble." We had a simple dinner with family and close friends. We didn't send out invitations, and we didn't use a registry. We verbally mentioned things the young mother needed to the women of the church. The gifts were sent home with her, and she opened them by herself. We were hesitant to create too much of a party mood that might encourage wrong behavior in other young girls in our church. We tried to create a balance of helping the girl without rewarding her for bad behavior.

- Not long ago I gave a shower for an unmarried, pregnant girl who was the daughter of a friend. Although I knew the young father-to-be was a "complete and total loser" and the young girl had the judgment of an alley cat, I wanted to show my love and support for the grandmother-to-be. I spent all kinds of money on the food, worked myself into the ground cleaning and decorating my house, and then bought a beautiful gift. The girl barely grunted a less-than-sincere thank you. At that moment I had to remind myself that the gift of hospitality I extended was for the benefit of my friend (who couldn't have been nicer and more appreciative) and for the glory of God.

Because whether or not to give a baby shower for an unwed mother is indeed a challenge for many folks, the following response represents those women who admitted their hesitance to give a shower.

> I don't think I would participate in the shower unless there was some acknowledgment that a sin had been committed and there was fruit of repentance. Our church is actually in this situation and I'm not quite sure what will be done. The young man is a member of our church but the girl is not a Christian.

As I read this representative response, my heart prayed that the church women would use this opportunity to reach this young woman with the love of Christ. I prayed that they would choose to find a way to *love her in* and not push her out. The opportunity for good is so very great, especially since this young woman isn't a Christ follower. What a great chance to show her the love and mercy, the grace and forgiveness that is the heartthrob of Christ.

The world will know we are Christ's disciples by the fruit of our love.

When it comes to reaching out to those wounded by their own transgressions and mistakes, I don't think we have to fear standing in front of God on judgment day and having Him say to us, "I think you were too kind." Nor would we hear, "You were a little too quick to forgive, to offer grace, to extend mercy. I think you showed love too much and too often to sinners and those who were hurting." If that is a concern you have, relax. *We will never out-love, out-forgive, or out-mercy God.* In the words of a dear friend and very outspoken Southern lady, "God will never let us dirty rotten sinners ever put Him to shame when it comes to showing love." She is so right. Another friend put it this way, "Love has to be greater than the law. Otherwise I have to wonder if it's love at all."

One of my favorite verses is James 2:13: "For judgment will be merciless to one who has shown no mercy; mercy triumphs over judgment." There is no doubt that an unwed mother needs mercy and grace. If Jesus didn't condemn the woman caught in adultery (John 8), where is our place of judgment to be found in condemning this young woman? The Scriptures tell us that the way the world will know we are Christ's disciples is by the fruit of our love. The world is not duly impressed with how right we can be, neither is it awed by the correct doctrine we proclaim. Jesus said, "By this all men will know that you are My disciples, if you have love for one another" (John 13:35).

LOVE THEM BOTH

Two people enter the room
one of them seen, one in the womb
one of them speaks and one has no voice
which do we love?

We have no choice
but to love them both, mother and child
let her know, let her see your smile
tell her you care so that when she goes
she'll know in her heart,
she'll have no doubt
that you love them both, mother and child

And someday when they return to you
that's when you'll see what love can do
because they'll know in their hearts,
they'll have no doubt
that you love them both, mother and child[1]

Mercy triumphed over disappointment regarding an unplanned and untimely pregnancy in the lives of some friends of mine. After learning the heartbreaking news they would become grandparents before they became in-laws, they wrestled for a while with the sorrow, fought the urge to be judgmental, and decided to show their daughter the two things she needed the most in that hour—love and compassion. This was an especially trying time for the dad, and though the words weren't easy to say aloud, he took his daughter in his arms and said the tender words Steve captured in this lyric:

WE WILL LOVE THIS CHILD

We will love this child, my child
that grows inside of you
love is how God smiles, so love is what we'll do
a dream come true too early,
still can be a dream come true
we will love this child, my child
the little one in you

This was not my plan for you or me
but plans were made to change sometimes
if they have to be
this child will lead you on a journey,
to another place in time
but love will go there with you, and
you will find, yes, you will find
we will love this child that grows inside of you[2]

Another question posed to the women in my survey addressed responding to those who solicit money or help on the street. I included this question because a heart of hospitality often takes us out of the comfort of our homes and churches and leaves us facing difficult social situations and decisions.

> *How do you respond if an individual (a homeless person, for example), solicits help on the street by asking you for money?*

- Usually I pretend I don't see them.

- I offer to go get them some coffee or a sandwich.

- If I have some money, I give it to them. I know there are those who go and buy smokes or drink with it, but what they do with it is not my responsibility.

- I am careful about giving money to homeless people. Many times they use the money to support bad habits. There are safe places for the homeless to go to where they can be cared for in a more dignified way. I usually tell them to go the rescue mission or a nearby church for help. I'm not comfortable getting involved.

- If they're hungry, I give them food. If they need clothing, I buy it. I will help them find shelter or pay for shelter for a week.

- If I have change, I give it to them and tell them God loves them.

- I offer to buy them a meal at a local restaurant, if possible. I do give a small amount of money, if I have it.

- I may or may not give them money. It all depends on how I feel at the time. However, I do attempt to show them the way by telling them where help is available to them.

- I will go and get food from a restaurant and bring it back to them.

- I let the Holy Spirit guide me as to what to do or say.

- I usually give a small amount of money with a tract that tells them about God's love.

- I'll give them food, but I won't give them money.

- I carry around in my purse and car gift certificates for McDonald's or other quick food places. When someone asks for money, I give them enough to get something to eat.

Knowing the right thing to do when approached by a person on the street soliciting money or help is difficult. I remember one day when a woman came up to me in a parking lot. I had my little granddaughter with me, and it was raining. First, I felt threatened and vulnerable. I was immediately worried the beggar might be mentally unstable and try to hurt my granddaughter. The lady asked me for money, telling me she needed gas and had left her wallet at home. My daughter-in-law had just told me how she'd been approached the day before in this parking lot for the same reason. So I had an idea that this woman probably hadn't accidentally forgotten her purse. This was a systematic scam. This woman didn't realize the "mother hen" instinct in me. It was raining and she was keeping me from getting my little grandbaby in the car and out of the deluge. That day it was not difficult for me to say, "No. I'm very sorry, but I have to take care of this baby right now."

Did I feel guilty for not dropping everything to show hospitality to this woman? No, I did not. We can't always do everything. Not only did I need to take care of my granddaughter, my "discerner" and the information my daughter-in-law shared let me know this unknown woman had targeted me simply because I was busy doing something else. Being hospitable and wanting to do the loving thing doesn't mean we don't use wisdom and discernment when we're asked for help.

Not long after the incident with the lady in the parking lot, I was going to my car at another store. (Notice the pattern?) A man approached me and asked for money for gas. He too had left his wallet at home. According to him, there was no one who could help him get enough gasoline to get home, about 20 miles away.

I did something I will never do again. I suppose I was irritated to be the target of another possible scam so soon. I asked the man if I could look into his car and see his gasoline gauge to see if it really was on empty. He took me to his car, put the key in, and I stuck my head in and saw that the gauge indicated an empty tank. I told him to follow me to the nearest gas station. I went to the counter at the station's convenience store and told the clerk to put $5 worth of gas on the pump where the man's car was parked. I didn't pull out my credit card or give the begging man money. I told the clerk to not give the man any change—only gasoline.

When I walked by him to get into my car, the man wouldn't look at me, nor did he thank me. I think he was miffed I only gave him a small amount of fuel. Perhaps he thought I should have given him more. I left feeling like I'd helped him. If he was a con man, and perhaps he was, my conscience was clear.

Looking back, I think I was very foolish. The man could have mugged me when I went to his car. I don't regret giving the gas—just the foolishness of putting myself in harm's way.

You have not lived today until you have done
something for someone who can never repay you.

JOHN BUNYAN

Bread, Blankets, and Bibles

One night I noticed my son going through my linen closet and pulling out blankets. I asked Nathan what he was doing. He said he and a friend were going downtown to where the homeless congregated, and they were taking blankets, bread, and Bibles. He asked me if we had any Bibles that weren't being used. I went to the bookshelf and found several that had been presented to us as gifts. Some were very expensive, leather-bound translations. As I thought about it, I realized what a terrible waste to have Bibles just sitting around.

The spirit of hospitality jumped from my son to me. I looked for any blankets that weren't in use, Bibles that weren't being read, and food that wasn't being eaten. Along with the provisions we could gather at our house, Nathan and his friend went to a local store and bought fresh, hot loaves of French bread to pass out.

———————

When our hospitality comfort zone is stretched by the
challenging needs of someone hurting, there is one
truth that will provide the motivation we need: No matter
how broken or abused a person appears, he or she
is worth whatever effort or investment we make.

———————

I was so proud of my son and his friend. Their intentions were to share the gospel with those who needed it desperately, but they also recognized that the people had other needs as well. Nathan was taking the gift of hospitality to the streets.

What are some things we can do to lend a hand to the homeless and those in need of help without jeopardizing our safety?

- Give money or time to a local rescue mission.
- Instead of handing out cash, carry gift certificates to fast-food restaurants and give them to those who ask for food.
- Carry granola bars and bottles of water or fruit juice to give to those soliciting food.
- Donate to the local Salvation Army.
- Participate in your church's outreach program. "Room in the Inn," for example, is a ministry where some congregations bring men and/or families from the street into their church during the cold months of the year. The guests are provided food, a hot shower, clean clothes, and a place to sleep overnight. The people of the church take turns staying overnight with them, making sure they are safe, they have the things they need, and the church people and building stay safe.

When our hospitality comfort zone is stretched by the challenging needs of someone hurting in our family or by seeing to the needs of those who struggle in the streets, there is one truth that will provide the motivation we need: No matter how broken or abused a person appears, he or she is worth whatever effort or investment we make. This e-mail by an anonymous author was sent to us by a friend in South Carolina:

> If I were to offer you a $20 bill, would you want it? Of course you would! However, if before I gave it to you I wadded it up tightly until it was wrinkled and ugly and lacked its original crispness, would you still want it? Of course you would. If I

also dropped it on the floor and stepped on it with the sole of my dirty shoes, would you still want the abused $20 bill? Of course you would. Why would you still want it? Very simply, the bill hadn't lost any of its value.

What a beautiful picture of how God views people. Though we may be tattered by life, wrinkled by trouble, and soiled by things we've done or things that have been done to us, we haven't lost one cent of value in God's merciful and loving eyes. He sees even the least of those among us as treasures and encourages us to do the same.

11

Grandmas, Grandkids, and Hospitality

Well, I can't say I wasn't warned. I'd been told by very reliable sources that the reward of not killing my children when they deserved it, was that they may someday reproduce and give me the indescribable gift of grandchildren. Oh, how right they were! All the flowery homilies can't come close to explaining how wonderful having the next generation within arm's reach can be.

Most of the time grandchildren are a tremendous blessing. Years ago I heard the little diddy, "I love the lights of Paris, I love the lights of Rome, but the lights I love the most—are the taillights I see when my grandchildren are going back home." Yes, no matter how much we love our grandchildren, they can be quite the test to our old backs, bad knees, and short fuses during extended periods of time...or for just a day sometimes. (I have a standing appointment with a chiropractor—it helps.) There are days that by the time my grandchildren leave my house I feel like I need to call an ambulance and get a transfusion of something—anything—that will restore my energy level.

With that said, let's not let the awesome opportunity of spending time with our children's children pass us by.

When I look at my grandchildren I feel a little like Moses must have when he stood on Mount Nebo looking down into the Promised Land. God said to him, "I have let you see it with your eyes, but you shall not go over there" (Deuteronomy 34:4). Knowing that we can influence the next generation in a positive way should motivate us to regard our time with our grandchildren as opportunities to invest in their lives and influence them to love and serve God.

If we're blessed enough to live close to our grandkids, hosting them in our homes is a much more productive use of our fleeting moments than playing another round of golf with our buddies or another bridge game with our friends. Our lives can have a greater purpose.

Several years ago, when our children were small, Steve described his role as a dad from a hunter's point of view and quipped, "As parents, we are the bow and our kids are the arrows that we launch into the future. Where they go and how effectively they fly is something to seriously consider." Today, as a granddad, he adds, "Now that our kids have kids, my job is to do what I can to encourage them as they pull taut the string of their parental bow from which their children will someday be sent. My folks did it for me, now it's my turn to help out."

The Eternal Influence of a Grandparent

Stories of godly, influential grandparents are peppered throughout the Scriptures, but few are more revered than the grandmother of Timothy. The apostle Paul's warm, endearing words to his young protégé give credit to the heritage of Timothy's faith: "I thank God, whom I serve with a clear conscience the way my forefathers did, as I constantly remember you in my prayers night and day, longing to see you, even as I recall your tears, so that I may be filled with joy. For I am mindful of the sincere faith within you, which first dwelt in your grandmother Lois and your mother Eunice, and I am sure that it is in you as well" (2 Timothy 1:3-5). Later Paul says, "You, however, continue in the things you have learned and become convinced of, knowing from whom you have learned them; and that from childhood you have known the sacred writings which are able to give you the wisdom that leads to salvation through faith which is in Christ Jesus" (2 Timothy 3:14-15).

Paul readily attributes the foundational faith Timothy possessed to the influence of the two main women in his life, his grandmother and his mother. The void that may have existed in Timothy's life (his father is never mentioned by name, basically all we know is that he was a Gentile) is evidently overcome by the time, teaching, and diligent instruction given by his mother and grandmother. Timothy's knowledge of Old Testament scriptures opened his heart to receive the gospel message of the risen Christ that Paul was preaching. Upon the foundation those lovely women carefully laid, the apostle Paul later helped build Timothy's life and ministry, in essence becoming the young man's spiritual father.

Appreciated or Abused?

While some grandparents relish the idea of spending time with their grandchildren, not everyone feels that way. When I was writing my book *The Mother-in-Law Dance,* I surveyed and interviewed hundreds of mothers-in-law and daughters-in-law. It wasn't uncommon during conversations concerning the complexities of the in-law relationship that the subject of grandchildren and the appropriate connection with their grandparents came up. Here are some of the complaints the grandmothers had:

- Sometimes I feel like I'm nothing more than a 24-hour, free babysitting service; a place for the grandchildren to be dumped.

- Sometimes I feel that my time and personal interests are being disregarded, and what I have planned for my day isn't important. I feel imposed upon.

- I have completed the job of raising children, and I have no intention of starting over with my grandkids. I resent being made to feel guilty or unloving because I don't want to keep my grandchildren all the time.

- Rearing children is best suited for younger people. I don't have the energy, the heart, or the mind to tackle that job again. When I visit with the grandchildren, I want their parents to be there so they can make them obey.

- The greatest pain in my life is having my precious grand-children withheld from me. I feel like those innocent little ones are being used as a form of control and manipulation by their parents. My heart is broken by being deprived of the opportunity to know and spend time with my children's children.

The relationship between a grandparent and a grandchild is an awesome privilege, and the lines of communication need to be nurtured. Admittedly, there are some grandparents who want their "own lives" and thus limit their exposure to their grandchildren. However, there are more who see their roles in the lives of their grandchildren as an awesome opportunity to show love for them and to provide an additional positive influence.

For the most part (I sure wish I could say it's true in all cases), grandparents simply want to spend time and invest in the lives of their grandchildren—not for the purpose of usurping or taking over the role of the parents, but to partner with them and help in any way they can.

Making Time, Making Memories

For some of us who work full-time or who have time-consuming hobbies and interests, it can be difficult to carve out blocks of time to host our grandkids and give them what they need and deserve. With my busy singing and speaking schedule, I know firsthand that I have to sacrifice something—even something I deem important—to create the time necessary for a strong relationship with my grandkids. For instance, I am an avid gardener. Until the arrival of my first grand-daughter, Lily, I spent as much as four to five hours a day when I was home during the growing season working in my various gardens. However, when Lily was born I realized something had to go. Since my work schedule wasn't flexible or optional, I had to give up something else to be with and show hospitality to my tiny little visitor. With the help of Steve, the two of us turned my lovely, carefully manicured English garden into a lush lawn. I said, "If I'm going to spend my time tending a flower, it's going to be a Lily." Although I miss the beautiful carpet of colorful flowers right outside my sunroom door, nothing compares to watching my sweet granddaughter blossom into a wonderful child of God.

What a joy to call Heidi and ask, "When can I keep Lily overnight?" or "When is a good night for you and Emmitt to have a date?" I'm blessed by my granddaughter's presence and contributing to the welfare of Heidi and Emmitt's marriage by helping take care of their children.

Although my garden dimensions have been dramatically reduced, I still manage to grow a few containers of bold and beautiful annuals. However, instead of my flower garden being a place of quiet solitude, it's become a classroom of learning for my little horticulturist. I call Lily my "flower girl." She has her own miniature watering can, a large brimmed straw hat, and little pink, princess garden shoes.

Along with watering and picking the flowers, her favorite job is to fill all the birdbaths with fresh water. I love spending time with her in the great outdoors. With the arrival of her baby sister, Josie, I will gladly make room for one more little watergirl.

Using hospitality to show love and serving my grandchildren is also another way I can love my children. When Steve and I were raising Nathan and Heidi we lived 400 miles from any close family. As a result, we had very little help with our kids. I know how it feels to need a break and not have family close by to chip in. I'm blessed that my kids live in the same town as Steve and me. What a joy to call Heidi and ask, "When can I keep Lily overnight?" or "When is a good night for you and Emmitt to have a date?" I'm blessed by my granddaughter's presence and contributing to the welfare of Heidi and Emmitt's marriage by helping take care of their children. Such a sacrifice!

Special Suggestions

My sister Alice is a special gift to this world. She was an activist long before I knew there was even "a cause." She makes an enormous difference in our home state of West Virginia as she tackles social and political ills. Among her fellow "world changers" with whom she has served in a variety of positions is Nancy D. Myers. When Alice learned that I was writing about hospitality she immediately suggested I contact Nancy and ask her to share her thoughts on showing hospitality to grandchildren.

Nancy is a very accomplished and busy woman. Her extensive career includes work in radio, newspaper publishing, and real estate. She's active in local, state, and national politics. She's also the mother of 4 daughters and the grandmother of 13 grandchildren! She definitely speaks with the voice of experience. Here's what she shared:

> My husband and I do very ordinary things with our grandchildren. Since our daughters work outside the home, we utilize our time with our grandkids to help them develop into wonderful citizens of both this world and the next. When the grandchildren are with us, we take them where they need to go: sports events, music lessons, doctor appointments, after-school activities. We willingly and with great joy try to help take the pressure off our children by assisting them with their children. I believe all three generations are benefiting by this arrangement.
>
> Generally we are home during the summer when the grandkids are out of school. This gives us a lot of time to spend with them. Their presence doesn't prohibit us from doing what we need to do. We take them with us when we go to the store, pay bills, or even take trash to the dump. Every activity allows us to teach them and welcome them into our adult world. Whether the grandchildren are helping my husband work on the car or helping me crack nuts on the patio, they contribute to our lives as much as we give to them.

My husband and I have the time to teach them things they need to know. I have taught them the proper way to set a table and divide up the recyclable items for the trash. My husband has spent a lot of time, especially with the boys, working in the tool shop or in the garden. Sometimes we prepare a simple picnic lunch and go to a nearby park where they can run and play. We are blessed to live in a small community where the grandchildren are safe and free to play outside. Kids need a chance to be kids without adults hovering over them every minute.

We don't feel it is necessary to constantly "entertain" our grand-children. Occasionally we might relax and watch a television show together, but that is the exception. During the summer months there's so much to be done, most of our time is spent outside.

The children love the feeling of helping us. They work in the garden with their grandfather and they explore nature. They exercise their imaginations as they spend time in the playhouse or join us in what-ever work we're doing.

On rainy days, we might pull out a box of family photos, work puzzles, tell family tales, talk about ancestors, bake goodies, or even surprise their parents with a special dinner the kids helped cook.

We keep plenty of fresh fruit, sandwich materials, and soups available for the children to eat. On the nights when their mommies have to work late, we feed the children dinner, assist with homework, help them sew special costumes if they're needed, and offer advice on school projects. Along with loving our grandchildren, we are giving hands and feet to the love we have for their parents.

One thing we do not do is worry about providing a lot of material things for our grandchildren. Of course we do spend a lot of money on gasoline and food for them, and that doesn't bother us at all. But we don't spoil the children with toys, gadgets, and unnecessary stuff. I would much rather the grandchildren learn to entertain themselves in creative ways rather than cluttering their world with things.

While we don't spoil our grandchildren with "stuff," we also don't ruin them by giving them full reign over us. We have do's and don'ts that we expect them to honor. A few of the basic rules are:

- Don't run in the house.
- Don't take food out of the kitchen (unless authorized to do so).
- Close doors. Do not slam them.
- Don't climb young trees.
- Don't go into other people's homes without our permission.
- Never leave the premises without permission.
- Do show respect for private property and their parents' and others' feelings.
- Keep your words kind and truthful.

We are not in competition with our children for our grandchildren's affection. Rather, we are partnering with their parents in the rearing of wonderful, loving, productive, secure, and creative individuals. My husband and I don't feel the least bit burdened with the fact that the grandchildren come over to our house a lot. I do not feel inconvenienced or like I'm sacrificing my life to be with them. The time we spend with the next generation is our choice, not a requirement. I deliberately have as my goal that my 13 grandchildren will have wonderful memories of our time together. I want them to remember all the love that was freely given to them by their grandparents.

Running the Race; Passing the Torch

Steve and I share Nancy and her husband's burning desire to influence the next generation. Giving hospitality is a natural and effective way to do that. We invite our grandchildren into our homes and into the busyness of our daily lives. Although Steve and I have invested our entire careers seeking to build up Christian families and encourage young couples across the world to put their families first, we both know that isn't enough. We must help our own children and our children's children do the same. That is only accomplished by spending time with them.

The influence grandparents have on grandchildren is a
direct result of their willingness to spend time with them.

In the Scriptures, the life of a Christ follower is depicted as a race that is to be run with purpose and endurance. In ancient times an athlete who entered a race was expected to not only run the distance and finish the course, but he was to run holding a lighted torch high in the air for all to see. The winner of the race was not only the one who crossed the finish line first, but the one who crossed the line *with his torch still burning.* As parents, our race includes the goal of a good finish, and we're also responsible to pass the baton of light on to the next generation. For there to be a smooth exchange between the two participants, they have to be close enough to reach one another. Sadly that closeness is missing in many families. In the stress and busyness of modern-day times, the generations bypass one another. Grandparents can help fill the gaps that may exist.

The contributions by both sets of our parents in the lives of our children is immeasurable. These incredible individuals demonstrated through the years what it means to be people of character and integrity. The influence they've had on our children is a direct result of their willingness to spend time with them.

Heidi has verbalized on many occasions the strength she's drawn from her relationship with her grandparents. She said, "Whenever I face a tough decision or am having a difficult day, I keep in mind that I have the blood of generations of strong women running through my veins. I can do what I need to do and I can be who I need to be because of the women who have shown me how to do it."

The resolve to do the job of being a wife and mother to her best ability was expressed in the following song lyric Heidi wrote. The struggles of a full-time, stay-at-home mom are not for the weak of heart. Her determination to do the job does me proud.

HOME IS SOMEWHERE

Well, it's goodnight again, little Lily
I hope you sleep tight
I'll be there in the morning
when you see the light
then it's one more time to the kitchen
and empty that sink
feels like the same old same old
then I start to think

I could be wrapping up a deal
or finishing a show
Getting ready for a downtown meeting
or teaching what I know
then others might say, "She's really going somewhere."
but I know where my heart will be when I get there
home is somewhere I want to run to
it's who I am, not just what I do
and when it feels like I'm going nowhere
then I remember home is somewhere

Well, I put away the last dish and dry my hands
I take a moment for myself
I do it when I can
and when it's me and my thoughts
and it's quiet in the house
I think of the one upstairs
And I have no doubt
that home is somewhere I want to run to[1]

It's hard to explain how much I can miss the presence of my grand-children in our home. (And may God bless those of you who are raising your grandkids.) While it might be right that grandchildren be our guests, Steve did a good job explaining the emptiness when the house is too quiet and could use the pitter-patter of little feet.

LILY ANNE

Lily Anne, you know I am so glad you came
My heart smiles every time I say your name
And when I know you're coming over
The waiting's hard to do
But the aching in my arms
Will go away when I hold you

Lily Anne, take my hand
Let's make some tea
And when it's made we'll find some shade
Just you and me
I'll be a king and you can be
A fancy Southern belle
We'll talk about your mama
I have some stories I can tell

And I've often wondered why they call it grand
But since you've come along, now I understand
Sweet Lily Anne[2]

Instead of mourning their necessary absence, I've decided to do something that you might want to do too. Especially when you feel the same ache for a grandbaby's presence. Since I can't always have them in our house, I can always host them in my heart. And the very best way to serve them in my heart is to pray for them as often as possible.

Long before we knew whether our first grandbaby was a boy or girl, Steve and I cried out to the Lord, "Father, bless every cell of baby Beall!" (Being musicians, we appreciate the rhyme—Beall is pronounced "bell.") That same prayer continues with each addition to the Chapman family. I encourage you who are blessed to have grandchildren to invest your time, your hospitality, your resources, and even more important, your prayers on their behalf.

Our children are privileged to have the prayer support of their grandparents. Of all the things they've done to bless their grandchildren, and now their great-grandchildren, the most important is their commitment to pray. The following lyric indicates one way Steve's mother loved her grandkids through the years.

WHEN I HEAR THAT TRAIN

Whenever I hear a train it takes me back
To where my Grandma lives near the railroad tracks
It was there she told me a long time ago
Child, I want you to know

You can be sure as long as I'm around
Every time I hear that train comin' through our town
I'm gonna bow my head and close my eyes
And I'm gonna lift my hands up to the sky

And pray for you
When I hear that train comin' through
I'll pray for you
That's what I'm gonna do
God's gonna hear your name
Every time I hear that train comin' through
I'm gonna pray for you

The time and the dreams took me away
From that little town, but it's still there today
And I'm thanking God there ain't no rust upon those rails
And the promise Grandma made for God never fails[3]

Most likely some of us are busy showing hospitality to all sorts of folks who cross our paths. We do so with the knowledge that we may be entertaining heavenly angels without knowing it. However, we can be sure as we entertain our grandchildren that we are indeed tending to some little angels—even when they act less than angelic. We must redeem the time and take advantage of every occasion to be with those "living arrows" that will be sent into the future. They carry our lineage, and they carry our hearts.

12

The Mt. Everest of Party Planning — the Wedding

There is no question that the granddaddy of all parties and the biggest challenge to hospitality skills is preparing for a wedding. Tackling that project can totally consume a person. Heidi and Emmitt got engaged in November. The wedding was scheduled for Thanksgiving weekend the next year. About two weeks after they announced their engagement I had a nightmare about the big event. I had no reservations about Heidi's intended groom; all my worries centered around how I was going to plan and execute a wedding with my heavy work schedule. To complicate matters, Heidi was still in college and wouldn't be able to help as much as she wanted to.

After experiencing yet another nighttime terror about running out of meatballs at the reception, I earnestly started praying about my inability to trust God with all the wedding details. My anxiety was understandable, to a point, because this was going to be the largest party I had ever put together. I remember specifically praying, "Oh Lord, I'm obsessing over this wedding. I'm going to be a raving lunatic by the time next November comes. All I can think of is this wedding. I need You to help me get this off my mind." I will never forget the "still small voice" of the Lord I heard that day. What I believe I heard shocked me because I'd never thought that before. I'm sincerely confident it was the Lord who gently said, "It is not wrong that you are concerned with the details of the wedding. That's what we've been doing in heaven for the last 2,000 years. We've been planning a wedding."

At that moment the preparations took on a new and special meaning. The arrangements for the big day became a spiritual picture of what God, the Father, is preparing for His Son, the Lord Jesus, and His bride, the church (Revelation 19:7-10). Everything we would do for Heidi and Emmitt's wedding would be a tiny picture of what is happening in heaven at this very moment. I felt a partnership with God in the preparations for the ceremony.

An extra-special comfort I received while asking God to help me sort out the endless details of planning a wedding was unique to my need for consolation in the hour of my "trial." God must have known I needed it! It was a revelation about my mother.

At that time my mom had been in heaven for three years. When the Lord told me that heaven is a-buzz, preparing for the biggest, most glorious wedding ever, everything fell into place for me. All of a sudden I could see my mom helping with the festivities. Mom was born and raised on a farm. She and my dad worked side by side making a living and sharing a life together for 52 years, so when I thought about my mother and my notion of what heaven was like, I couldn't imagine her floating around on a cloud and doing nothing. She was a hard-working woman who didn't waste time. I'd always wondered what mom was doing in heaven. After the Lord spoke to me and said that heaven is planning a wedding, I now picture what she's been doing all those years. I know in my heart that she is preparing for a wedding and making potato salad.

Steve has warned me about adding to the Scriptures, and I'm aware that nowhere in the Bible does it say that people are cooking in heaven, but humor me. My mother loved to go to weddings. And she had a rather interesting gauge she used to tell if the wedding was really successful or not. She'd come home from the festivities and say, "Wasn't that a nice wedding? Did you taste the potato salad?" Or she would say, "That wedding wasn't anything to brag about. They didn't even have potato salad." So I couldn't help but chuckle out loud when the thought came that if there is potato salad on the menu of the marriage feast of the Lamb, my mother is probably in charge of it. Her potato salad was the best.

After that conversation with God about the wedding preparations and the seemingly divine revelation about my mother, I felt released to pursue excellence with gusto in our little earthly picture of a heavenly happening.

Ideas for a Blessed Wedding

I'm not a wedding expert, and there are lots of people much more versed on the do's and don'ts of nuptial affairs. But in planning Heidi's wedding and helping with Nathan's, I came up with some helpful ideas that served me well. If you're in the midst of planning a wedding, perhaps some of these ideas will help you complete your unique and special mission.

The first thing I did was buy a large accordion folder that went everywhere I went as Heidi and I planned the event. Inside the large folder were individual files labeled for each thing we needed.

The first item on the list was invitations.

Invitations

Who will be invited to the wedding and reception and when those invitations should be sent out was our first priority. Use a folder to help you keep on schedule. Gather samples of invitations, create a realistic budget, write down names and addresses of those to be invited.

Compiling names with respective addresses can be quite a chore. Start well in advance in getting this information. By all means have the groom get started on his list as soon as possible. You may have to remind him often about getting it done.

On the outside of the file folder was a list of jobs and dates for them to be completed. As they were completed a check mark was placed in the box (and there was much celebration!). Some of the jobs that needed to be done were:

- appointment to look at invitation samples
- date the invitations should be ordered
- date when the invitations needed to be addressed and sent. (A sweet friend who had beautiful penmanship was enlisted to help with addressing the envelopes.)
- a tally of the number of attendees needed to be sent to the caterer

Periodically I would sit down and review the file, making sure we were keeping up on the deadlines.

When the invitations were ordered we included response cards with envelopes. We had my address imprinted on the response envelope and stamped each one. When the responses were sent back to us, we kept the ones for those who were planning on attending in a large ziplock bag for easy reference. Money receipts for the invitations, stamps, and related items were also kept in the folder.

Programs for the Ceremony and Reception

Heidi and I were grateful when Emmitt's family volunteered to take on the important responsibility of producing handouts that would be given to the guests. All I had to do was collect the pertinent information and send it to them. Since the order of events and most of the other particulars that needed to be in the program weren't available until the week of the wedding, this was a last-minute project that could have stressed me out.

Marriage is a threefold living relationship between a man and a woman and their God. The guests are present to witness and affirm the union. They are an integral part of the ceremony and should be included as much as possible.

Wedding programs are handy to have so guests can know what's coming and identify the people who are involved. I like to know who is presenting the special music, the name of the songs, the names of the attendants and their relationships to the bride and groom. Knowledgeable guests are more emotionally engaged in the ceremony and more conscious of what is happening.

In the midst of the planning and details, it is easy to lose perspective on what is really happening. A wedding isn't a show. It documents the establishment of a holy covenant between the couple and the God of the universe. Marriage is a threefold living relationship between a man and a woman and God. The guests are present to witness and affirm the union. They are an integral part of the ceremony and should be included as much as possible.

Photography and Videography

Choosing the photographer and/or videographer who will fulfill expectations is an important part of the planning. This person or persons will document for years to come the fruit of the commitment of the couple and the effort put forth for the wedding. Keeping abreast of all the details for photographing and videotaping can be daunting. This file folder helped me keep up-to-date on deposits and contracts. When I talked to the photographer, I kept my file close by. Any changes were written down and dated, as well as the particulars of that conversation. A word of advice: Don't trust your memory. There are far too many details.

Not taking the time to find a photographer or spending the money to have good pictures taken at our wedding is one regret Steve and I share. We were married in the heyday of the hippie movement. One of the rules of a card-carrying hippie was to embrace simplicity. This way of thinking sadly carried over into our attitude about posing for pictures. In a misguided desire to be "real," we thought that if a picture wasn't a candid, live shot, totally spontaneous and without pretense, it wouldn't be authentic. So we resisted the idea of having formal photos. As a result we have only a handful of snapshots that some friends and family took. If we could do it over, we would spend the bucks to have a professional, well-respected photographer employed for the day.

Beautiful Dresses

When Heidi was wedding dress shopping I took along a camera. I documented every dress she tried on. It was so much fun at the time, and now it's even more fun to look back over the dresses that didn't make the grade.

In this file folder are the pictures and receipts for the wedding dress, veil, and special undergarments. Also included are ideas for the bridesmaid dresses torn from magazines and catalogs. Since we had a dressmaker do the sewing, we also have dress patterns, samples of material, and proposals for cost.

Whenever I talked to the seamstress about any changes that needed to be made, set a fitting date, or discussed alterations for the bridesmaid dresses, I carefully documented all communication. It was great having everything in one place, and keeping detailed notes helped avoid any misunderstanding. I also gave a copy of my notes to the seamstress to make sure we were on the same page. Never leave anything to memory—yours or those with whom you're working.

The Ceremony Location

The church we were attending at the time was on the small size, considering all the folks Heidi and Emmitt wanted to invite. So we checked out several churches that were available. Each church we scheduled to see allowed us to take pictures of their facilities. We then compared them at home for a more unbiased perspective.

When we settled on the church and the arrangements were made to secure the building, we were then asked to work with their wedding coordinator. My folder came in handy because it helped me keep up with the arrangements, when the church could be accessed, phone numbers to call if we had a problem, and the rules for use and cleanup.

Delicious Food

Keeping a folder on the menu possibilities, prices, and related expenses was also crucial. Food is one of the details that deserves and demands a lot of attention. I soon realized that the gift the guests brought was their presence at the wedding. Our gift to them was providing an excellent meal for them to enjoy.

At first I thought it was silly for us to provide a banquet of food to feed people who could very easily feed themselves. Why should we spend all that money on something that wasn't necessary? I knew from personal experience that we didn't have to have a big, fancy wedding to get married. When Steve and I got married in 1975, we had a simple, meaningful, cheap wedding. The whole event cost us $200. That price included my $30 dress and $2 shoes. Yep, the whole hippie thing again. I wore flowers in my hair, and Steve donned a homemade shirt made from unbleached muslin material. Along with our pared down wedding duds, our wedding menu was just as simple. In fact, it never crossed our financially strapped minds that we should feed a complete meal to our 125 guests. A simple cake, peanuts, mints, and fruit punch were served and seemed to be plenty.

Things have changed in the last 30 or so years, and expectations have evolved with them. However, it wasn't until I began to study the whys behind some of the things we do at weddings that I found peace with the feasting part of the celebration. I learned that one of the meanings of the word "covenant" is "to feed." Feeding our guests was not only a lovely way of thanking them for taking their valuable time and coming to share something that was very important to us, but it was also a way for them to actively participate in the ceremony itself.

After discovering this, I joyfully and with grateful appreciation planned the food for the reception. And yes—there was potato salad at the reception! There was plenty of it, and it was as close to my mother's recipe as I've ever gotten.

Flowers

Because flowers can represent quite a hefty portion of the cash outlay for a wedding, keeping a folder on all things related to the florist was unbelievably important. There were many choices and expenses related to decorating and adorning the church and reception hall. I could never have kept track of the deposits and deadlines associated with the florist without my nifty filing system.

Furnishing and Equipment Rentals

When dealing with rental stores have a clear understanding of what has been decided. We rented chairs, tables, the punch fountain, and several other items. Having everything in writing eliminated any misunderstandings of what was to be delivered and by what time and date. Three days before the wedding I called to remind them of the date of delivery and pick up, as well as the various items we were expecting. They have lots of clients; we only had one wedding. Even though they probably didn't need to be reminded, I chose to be safe. Even though it cost a little more (and the extra expenditure did not go unnoticed), we paid to have the rental company bring the items to the church and pick them up after the event. The last thing we wanted to do the day after the wedding was load tables and chairs and take them back to the rental store. As Steve said about much of the spending for the wedding, "It was worth every dime I'll never see again."

Thanking the Bridesmaids, Groomsmen, Shower Hosts, and More

Buying gifts for the many people involved in a wedding is a very nice thing to do, and I considered it a necessity, but it did add to the budget. I was excited to find a store that was going out of business. Everything was 75 percent off the marked down price! I bought four items for what one would originally cost me. I was able to purchase the hostess gifts for those who helped give bridal showers for Heidi. I also found in the store Heidi's china pattern. I purchased at a pocketbook-friendly discounted rate some dishes for her. I left the store loaded down with lovely items at rock-bottom prices. What a thrill to walk into the bridal showers and present a beautiful host gift to each one who was showering love on my daughter.

A friend of mine traveled often to Turkey. She told me that many of the women with whom she worked made lovely handcrafted jewelry with high-quality silver. I told her to keep her eyes open for bridesmaid gifts. On one of her trips she came back with exquisite silver and pearl necklaces she'd purchased at reasonable prices. The money exchange at the time favored the U.S. dollar.

The key to finding the best deals and acquiring the best gifts was planning far in advance. I saved a lot of money and was able to give wonderful gifts on Heidi's behalf.

Helping the Attendants

The night before the wedding, at the rehearsal dinner, I gave the attendants file folders with all the information they might need for the next day. In each folder was a detailed list, including:

- Expected time of arrival to the church the next day. I allowed for a 30-minute grace period. It's much better to tell them 30 minutes earlier than needed than to have them 15 to 20 minutes late and holding up the show.

- What time to be ready for the photographer.

- A map to the church, along with phone numbers of the church and the wedding coordinator.

- Suggestion that they eat before the wedding. I also noted that fruit, small sandwiches, cookies, and bottled water would be available in the dressing rooms. I didn't want anyone fainting from lack of nutrition.

- I even included a note that said, "About 20 minutes before the wedding is to start, go 'tinkle.' I don't want anyone needing to go to the bathroom while the ceremony is in process."

Along with this information, I gave those who were serving as attendants to the bride and groom a simple item that helped our organization efforts immensely. I went to the local discount store and purchased medium-sized cardboard boxes. I wrote the attendants' names on them and placed them in their dressing rooms. They were asked to keep all their belongings in it. I suggested they not only put their change of clothes and shoes in it, but also their blow dryers, curling irons, jewelry, brushes, makeup, and anything they brought with them to get ready for the wedding. At the end of the day, when it was time to clean the dressing rooms, all they had to do was pick up their boxes and place the lids on top. This simple setup kept confusion at bay when it was time to leave.

Meals and Lodging

When expecting a large number of out-of-town guests, it's very helpful to do some of the leg work for them. Figure an estimated number of guests, and call nearby motels or hotels to negotiate a group rate. If you have several choices, shop around. If one establishment offers you a rate for several rooms, call and see if a nicer hotel will match it or give a bigger discount. After securing the settled rate in writing (they can fax the agreed amount to you), contact the guests who are coming and give them the information, including the phone number, e-mail, and street address. Your guests can take it from there and secure and pay for their own rooms.

Heidi and Emmitt's wedding was scheduled for Thanksgiving weekend. The long holiday weekend made it possible for family and friends to attend the wedding who normally may not have because of distance. Because it was a holiday, I invited several of them who were going to be part of the wedding ceremony to come in early and share Thanksgiving dinner with us. This made the wedding weekend feel more like a weeklong celebration. And our family and friends had more time to visit!

To reduce my workload with all this company, one thing I did that I will never regret was enlisting outside help with housework and meal preparations. I knew Heidi was going to want to share her last "single days" with her lifelong girlfriends. They would go shopping, talk, drink lattes, and get manicures and pedicures. I also knew that I was going to desperately need help during the days leading up to the wedding, and the last thing I wanted to do was put stress on Heidi.

A few months earlier Heidi was an attendant at a wedding of one of her close girlfriends. I also attended, and when Heidi needed help with her dress I went into the dressing room. I was an inadvertent observer of an intense confrontation between the bride and her mother. The mom was expressing how upset she was that the young woman had let her down during the preparations for her wedding. Just minutes before the bride was to walk down the aisle, they were having words over the situation. My heart was broken over the scene, and I imagined what regrets they both were going to have after the stress and fatigue had subsided. The hot tears on the bride's face and the anger in the mother's voice alerted me to avoid this scenario.

Thankfully, I found a young lady in town who was trying to secure funds to fly home for Thanksgiving to see her parents, who lived 1500 miles away. Steve and I agreed to purchase her plane ticket in return for her help before and during the wedding. Together we made cookies, baked nut bread, created breakfast casseroles, and prepared the house for the many people who would be coming and going throughout the weekend.

On the night of the wedding rehearsal, this young woman came in after we left for the church and gathered up all the dirty clothes and towels that had been left in the bathrooms. (Many out-of-town family members used our house to get ready for the evening.) She washed, dried, folded, and put them away. She also loaded and ran the dishwasher, cleaned and swept the kitchen, and straightened anything that had been disrupted.

The evening was perfectly wonderful, just as I had imagined, thanks to having an assistant to help with all the work that had to be done.

What a blessing to come home from a long day of decorating,

rehearsing, and visiting to find a clean, orderly, warm, inviting house! It was just what I needed to make it through the rest of the weekend. Instead of scurrying around cleaning house and doing laundry, I was able to sit by the fire with my family and enjoy our company before everything erupted again in a flurry of activity.

Except for one exception, no out-of-town guests stayed in our house. (Not even my sisters, whom I love more than life itself.) I wanted only our immediate family at home those last few hours before our family changed forever (even if it was a great change!). The exception was Stephanie. Our son had told us he was going to propose to her the afternoon after Heidi and Emmitt departed for their honeymoon. Stephanie came in from Virginia to attend the wedding.

While we sat around the fire laughing and talking about the events of the day and anticipating the coming nuptials, I got out two gifts I had purchased for this special time.

I gave beautiful, soft bathrobes for the two young women. Stephanie's had a holiday theme, and Heidi's was a lovely white I knew would feel good on her honeymoon.

The evening was perfectly wonderful, just as I had imagined, thanks to having an assistant to help with all the work that had to be done.

The Reception

With so much attention given to the wedding ceremony, often the reception is an afterthought. Since I was in charge of the lion's share of the wedding preparations, I was more than glad to pass the responsibility of planning the reception to Steve. He helped make the reception a continuation of the festive morning wedding.

Steve asked a wonderful friend of ours, Ken Fletcher, to be the master of ceremonies. Ken's responsibility was to serve as coordinator and communicator. Throughout the afternoon the guests were kept informed as to what was going to be taking place.

Steve also called several of our musical friends who are dedicated to strengthening families and asked them to sing a song or two. We were blessed, as well as our many guests, by the musical talents offered by these people.

Finally, about 30 minutes before the bride and groom were to leave for their honeymoon, an announcement was made that the reception was coming to an end. We all gathered to send the newlyweds off in style. Guests who might have gone ahead and left stayed because they knew when the reception was going to be over. Too often the newly married couple have few guests to send them off because friends and family have already gone home. We thought it just as important to have an ending time to the reception as a beginning time.

The Loose Ends

Just a couple of final thoughts that might help you as you plan for this granddaddy of all parties. Often close friends say, "If there is anything I can do, just let me know." My response was always, "Do you mean that or are you just being nice?" After they recovered from my honesty, most generally said, "I really mean it. I really do want to help."

I was ready with a list of tasks that needed to be done. This was a tremendous help. There were a few beyond-the-ordinary tasks that got accomplished this way.

Because Heidi's wedding was at the beginning of the Christmas season, we decided to decorate the reception hall with lighted Christmas trees around the perimeter of the room. When various close friends and family asked what they could do I said, "If you really want to help, then bring a Christmas tree already decorated with white lights. Set it up in the reception hall the day before the wedding, and at the end of the reception, take it down and take it home." To my delight and the credit of our special guests, we had more than 15 Christmas trees that provided ambient light for the hall. The soft glow of white lights was the perfect touch.

Another friend, Melanie, is very artistic. She volunteered to use her creative abilities to make beautiful signs that alerted guests to the location of the reception hall and a nicely presented message that reminded guests to turn off their cell phones—even the vibrate function—so guests wouldn't answer their phones and leave the room during the celebration.

Final Thoughts Before I Get Some Needed Rest

Heidi's wedding was the apex of my hospitality offerings (so far anyway!). But, candidly, I couldn't have accomplished this challenging time had I not had the help of my family and friends. If you're facing this daunting but wonderful task, invite family and friends to help. Everyone will be blessed.

By the way, passing on this wedding information to help your planning and hosting was made much easier because everything I wanted to share was in the accordion folder. You gotta get one!

13

Santa Isn't the Only One Coming

Holidays and hospitality go together like coffee and cream and dogs and fleas. Without a doubt entertaining during the long Christmas holiday season can be the best of times and the worst of times. Regardless of the emotional, financial, and physical toll it takes, having company over the holidays can be wonderful...and the more, the better.

Part of the fun of this special time is creating memorable moments that will live long after the Christmas tree has been taken down, the fruit cake has been thrown away, and the seven pounds of weight gain has become a permanent part of our body landscape.

One particular Christmas memory never fails to make me laugh. My sister Gayle and her children, Billy and Allison, came for a visit. As she walked off the plane with her two-year-old son and three-month-old daughter, I could tell she was exhausted. Due to her husband's work schedule, he was going to join us later. After a nice afternoon of the adults visiting and the children taking a much-needed nap, we were excited to share our Chapman family Christmas traditions with them.

Gayle had brought some early Christmas gifts for our children. Nathan and Heidi were excited and could hardly wait for the "go" signal so they could tear into the bounty.

Before the children could open the gifts, however, Steve announced that our family had a "job" to do. During the year we were reading the One Year Bible and doing fairly well at keeping up with the prescribed schedule. With the busyness of the holidays, though, we had gotten a few days behind. Not wanting the kids to get the impression that toys were more important than the Word of God, Steve decided we were going to catch up before the children opened any gifts.

While this was a legitimate reason for pressing on with the reading, I suggested that another night might be better for a lengthy reading since the children were excited about having special company and gifts. But Steve was not to be deterred.

The daily portions of Scripture we had neglected were in the minor prophets. As Steve stood in the living room reading aloud the passages that were rather lengthy, the expressions on the faces of Nathan and Heidi turned from seasonal excitement to impatient scowls. Gayle's children began to fidget. The squirming of all the kids grew in intensity as the minutes dragged on. Steve's voice rose as he competed with the noise of the kids. Little Billy started a serious wailing of protest about being made to sit still on the couch. His sustained outburst caused him to choke and regurgitate. Baby Allison joined in with loud, piercing screams in reaction to her big brother's angst.

The seemingly endless Bible reading continued with Steve almost yelling to be heard above the din.

As Steve shouted Scripture above the sounds of the children, who were now screaming and pleading for mercy, he happened to be reading the Nahum passage where mayhem reigned, children were being dashed against the rocks, and blood ran down the streets. Steve, immersed in completing the reading, didn't notice what was happening—but Gayle and I did. The kids were providing a very convincing audio backdrop to the disturbing biblical drama that was being read. Gayle and I began to laugh uncontrollably. When we finally got Steve's attention and pointed the situation out to him, he bent over double in laughter as well—to our relief!

After a while we calmed down, and as we wiped tears of laughter from our eyes, my sister said, "So this is how the Chapmans celebrate the glorious birth of the Christ child. You read the book of Nahum!" Then the belly laughs began all over again...and they restart each time we recall that moment.

That evening with Gayle's family was a time of chuckling and upchucking. Why does the pendulum of emotion swing so wide during holidays? While some of the seasonal stress is unavoidable, much of it seems to be self-inflicted, as was the case in our unforgettable memory moment (which Steve owns up to now). I asked women these questions in a survey:

What is the most stressful part of holiday entertaining? What do you do to help prepare for the holidays and make them less stressful?

- My holiday season would be a lot more enjoyable if I had more time to prepare for my guests. I work right up to Christmas Day, so it's hard to enjoy having guests when I'm not ready and already exhausted.

- I can't find enough time to do all the things I want to do: decorating, baking, visiting, and entertaining.

- I find it exhausting to be a host—always on duty and being responsible for every meal and all the cleanup.

- The solution to many years of stress-filled holiday entertaining is to start early. Sometimes I start the week before Thanksgiving. I discovered that if I decorate a little at a time, over a longer period of time, it all gets done and I'm not stressed to the max.

- I've simplified my holiday decorations. Just because I have them, doesn't mean I have to put them all up.

- I swallow my pride and buy some of the holiday meal already prepared.

- I limit how many invitations I accept for parties and activities.

- The best stress-buster I've found is prayer. I pray that God will give me supernatural insights into which guest needs a little extra attention, what work needs to be done, and where I need to put my energy.

- The hardest part when I entertain overnight company is to make sure everyone is having a good time. I don't mind doing a lot of work, it's the "fun" part that stresses me out.

- I save up vacation time so I can get ready for my guests. My house usually looks like a tornado hit by the time my grandkids get through with it. After a day or two I stop trying to keep it neat.

- My company comes in waves. I love seeing all my family during the holidays, but it's difficult. One group leaves at one o'clock and the next arrives at three. Keeping up with the house is nearly impossible. I do well to change the sheets on the beds.

- I worry about the food for the holidays. I usually fix way too much, and then I end up throwing some away.

- Sometimes I get so involved with taking care of my out-of-town company that I neglect my children. It's hard to find the correct balance.

- From Thanksgiving through New Year's my healthy eating plan goes out the window. My company wants the fattening, sugary, tasty, unhealthy foods they're used to. That's what I fix them, and then I eat it too.

- Holiday entertaining breaks our budget. Not only does the food cost so much, but my washer and dryer never stop running. I love to have guests stay, but it hurts financially, and we're paying the bills long after they leave.

- I have lots of guests and few ideas. I don't know what to serve them to eat or how to entertain them while they are here.

- I try to please everyone and send everyone away with wonderful memories and lots of goodies. Do you think I'm stressed? You betcha.

- I love to have company during the holidays, but I don't want them to stay overnight. "Fish and company stink after three days," however, I think company begins to smell after three hours.

Hospitality's Most Lovely Decoration

Every magazine cover from October through December—or at least most of them—has something to do with the holidays. From the elegant table settings and the impressive menus to the exquisitely decorated trees, we are fed a fantasy of what the holidays are to look like and how we're supposed to feel. But the most important part of our holiday adornment has nothing to do with rare, hand-blown glass ornaments or expensive, carefully beaded garlands. The best part of Thanksgiving and Christmas dinners is not the delicious food or the creative centerpiece. The most important and most memorable part of our celebration meals is what happens *around* the table.

When we praise people in private it makes them
feel good. But when we praise them publicly it
makes them feel loved and respected.

A host has the responsibility to guide the tone, if not the subject, of the conversation at the table. Nothing ruins a lovely time with friends and family than inappropriate, crude conversation. As a host, I often prepare questions to ask my guests. Also, after the meal is finished, we go around the table and each person shares what has happened since our last gathering. We respectfully take turns giving each other opportunities to talk.

Last Christmas I hosted a gathering of seven couples. After the meal was complete, I asked each spouse to share something they appreciated about his or her mate. A wonderful time was had by all, and each person at the table went away feeling good about the evening. When we praise people in private it makes them feel good. But when we praise them publicly it makes them feel loved and respected.

Another question on my survey to women gives more insights into holiday hospitality:

Do you reach out to your neighbors during the holidays?

- Everyone seems so busy with their own families so I don't do anything for them.
- I reach out to others through my church but not to my neighbors.
- Yes, I give my neighbors Christmas cards and fruit baskets.
- I invite neighbors who don't have anywhere else to go to my house.
- I like to take meals and food to families who are in need.
- We give our neighbors wood for heat and provide food to others. I gave a woman in our church a winter coat I didn't need.
- Fortunately our neighborhood is pretty friendly. We have a community open house at the beginning of December. The women exchange gifts and the men play dominoes.
- Our family members are active military. There are a lot of single men and women unable to go home for the holidays so I always have a houseful for dinner. I also send boxes of cookies and goodies to deployed men and women we know.
- At Thanksgiving I usually make homemade bread and deliver it to my neighbors with a note saying, "We're thankful to have you in our neighborhood."
- This past Christmas our family, with my parents dressed as Mr. and Mrs. Claus, went to sing Christmas carols at a local retirement home.
- I make a point of inviting widows and widowers for Thanksgiving and Christmas dinner.
- I send Christmas cards.
- My husband is a contractor. He works with a lot of men who have no place to go for the holidays. We invite them to come to our home for a holiday dinner.

- I play the piano for nursing home residents in our community. They love the familiar Christmas songs.

- I wish I did, but I'm too busy.

- I take "one-dish" meals to my neighbors—spaghetti, home-made soup, chili, things like that.

- I make dinner on the Monday before Thanksgiving and invite my neighbors over. I want them to know I appreciate them.

Hos*pie*tality

The extended Chapman family often use the gift of hospitality during the Thanksgiving and Christmas seasons to reach out to others. Steve and I moved into the Nashville/Rosebank neighborhood the fall of 1977. Being new to the area, we wanted to get to know our neighbors. We thought the holiday season would be a good opportunity to extend our best wishes.

That first holiday season I made two homemade apple pies for each immediate neighbor. When Christmas came around the next year I did the same as I had before, but I added the neighbors across the street. Including additional neighbors continued through the years. The last year we lived in that particular neighborhood I made 33 pies from scratch. Along with the apple-laden pastry we included a card thanking each of them for being such good neighbors. With the children in tow we hand-delivered the desserts. This simple act of kindness opened doors to our neighbors and their hearts were opened to us. Those open doors were used to share God's love on many, many occasions.

Even after we moved from the Rosebank neighborhood, we continued to return each year, taking pies to our beloved friends. The holiday season offered us a chance to do things for our neighbors that might have been misunderstood in the middle of the summer. When cloaked in the spirit of the season, any speculation of ulterior motives is generally eliminated. We never sensed that our neighbors were silently asking, "Why are they doing this? What do they really want?" Our act of love was accepted for what it was—reaching out to them with the love of Christ.

Including the Neighborhood Kids

Our street was the playground for kids of all ages. Seeing the kid-filled street as an opportunity for sharing Christ, Steve and I decided we should seize the chance to teach and reach out to the children. We decided to produce a Christmas movie using them as the cast, including the various pets that roamed our cul-de-sac.

We armed ourselves with an old camcorder we bought at a yard sale and secured a supply of old sheets and towels. We went outside to recruit our participants. Choosing one of the preteen girls to play Mary and one of the young teenage boys to play Joseph, we explained the Christmas story to the children. The other youngsters were chosen to play the innkeeper, shepherds, and wisemen. We spent time dressing the tykes in the linens I brought from home. A neighbor's outbuilding was adorned with a large star covered in aluminum foil. The pets were arranged around the shed waiting for the arrival of the young couple. Mary and Joseph then went from house to house asking the neighbors if there was room in their hearts for Jesus.

Once the filming was complete we went home to watch the movie. Within the body of the film was the good news of Christ coming into the world to save us. Later we invited the parents and other neighbors to come over and watch our cinematic adventure with the children. I served doughnuts and hot chocolate.

Was the effort to bring the reality of Christmas to the kids in our neighborhood worth it? I couldn't think of a better use of our time. It was so enjoyable that I didn't even get upset that I had to clean up after the kids tracked mud and debris through the house. This movie experience left a positive and lasting effect on the neighborhood.

Our contact with the kids continued through the years. The following Christmas the children wanted to come to our house and watch the movie again. It was fun to see how much they'd changed. Taking our gift of hospitality to the street created delightful memories all around.

MYSTERY OF THE SEASON

I don't understand it, but it happens every year
It hits me in December, I get that longing to be here
It's like I'm one of the wisemen
And this house is like the star
Something inside me says, "Make that journey"
I can feel it in my heart

It sends me down the highway
To feed this hunger in my soul
I drove all day to get here
As if I had control
And the cars out in the driveway
Tell me I am not alone
It's the mystery of the season
One by one, coming home

Some cross the streets to get here
Some come from distant shores
Some arrive in their latest success
Some arrive in rusty Fords
One may come in anger
One may choose to stay away
If they do, I think I know how they'll
Spend their holiday

I believe the saddest day I'll ever spend
Is yet to come
It's when it's time to make this journey
But all the reasons to are gone

But it sends me down the highway
To feed a hunger in my soul
I drove all day to get here
As if I had control
And the cars out in the driveway
Tell me I am not alone
It's the mystery of this season
One by one, coming home[1]

14

In Bad Times and Good Times

It was four-thirty in the morning when everyone should be sleeping. My (Heidi) in-laws, the Bealls, were awake and lacing up their running shoes. Why would a houseful of sane people be doing such a thing on a holiday morning? *Tradition.* Every year my husband's family gets up at the crack of dawn on the Fourth of July to run a 10k race through downtown Atlanta. The odd thing is almost 50,000 other supposedly sane people are doing the same thing! The Peachtree Road Race is a long-standing runners' delight.

While Emmitt and I were dating I decided to run the six mile race with them. Let me say up front that I am not a runner, I don't want to be a runner, I will never be a runner. I was and am, however, a smitten and in-love woman, so I was willing to endure an hour and a half of sheer torture to impress Emmitt's family. I did this until a couple of years into our marriage. I decided I'd run my last "to impress" mile. So last year, at the same time their eager feet were hitting the pavement, I was hitting the snooze button.

When I did arise, I slowly shuffled to the kitchen to get my much-needed java fix. I noticed a handwritten note on the coffeemaker that read "Just push the button." Someone had prepared the coffeemaker for me. All I needed to do was turn it on. I was thrilled that I didn't have to make my morning drug; it was ready to go. It wasn't until after the sweaty, exhausted runners returned that I learned my coffee hero's identity. Emmitt's father, Emmitt Sr., had done the good deed. My father-in-law, even at such an early hour, knew my need for caffeine and took the time to prepare everything. I felt very loved. I decided at that moment to pass that blessing on to someone else.

Not long after that a longtime pal of my mom's was coming to Nashville to visit her daughter, who was in the hospital having surgery after a near-fatal car accident. Susan would be staying in town while her youngest child recovered. My mom learned of Susan's visit and quickly offered their home. The catch, though, was mom and dad would be out of town at the time of Susan's unexpected visit. That's where I came in.

Isn't it amazing how one small act of hospitality can make such a difference in someone's day?

Mom called and asked me to drive to her house and make it ready for overnight company. I didn't mind; I knew there wouldn't be much to do. I have a very neat and tidy and organized mother. I assumed that even though she left town not expecting an overnight guest, her home would be just a few tweaks away from being "company ready."

On my way to the "Chapman Bed and Breakfast" I stopped to pick up a few things at the market. I bought cereal, milk, fruit, cookie dough, and coffee. When I arrived at mom's house it was just as I had predicted. I made sure there were clean towels in the guest bath and fresh sheets on the bed. I set up the breakfast options on the counter and baked the deliciously decadent cookie squares. I also filled the coffeemaker with water and coffee grounds. I placed a note with instructions covering what was available for breakfast to how to work the TV remote, which I put beside the platter of fresh, home-baked cookies. At the bottom of the paper I wrote, "About the coffeemaker—just push the button. It's ready to go." I was thrilled that I could bless someone the way Emmitt Sr. had blessed me.

After the weekend passed my mom got a beautifully written thank-you note from Susan. In the letter she mentioned how wonderful it was that she didn't have to make the coffee. Even though it is normally considered a small job, after being in the hospital all day and waiting for doctors' reports, she was so spent emotionally she wasn't sure she could have handled even such a mundane chore. Isn't it amazing how one small act of hospitality can make such a difference in someone's day?

What else can you and I do to bless people experiencing trials? What are the common threads of hospitality that can be used in nearly every situation?

Giving Comfort Through Actions

The brands of hospitality that come easiest for me are planning parties, hosting afternoon teas, and entertaining overnight guests in my home. What is not so second nature is reaching out when sadness and grief are involved. Sometimes I wish the gift (and commandment!) of showing God's love to others is as simple as having the nearest caterer on speed dial, but most of the time it is so much more than that. Blessing others requires a constant determination to serve in whatever way they might need and to do so without complaining if it doesn't exactly fit into our preference for entertaining. First Peter 4:9-11 admonishes us to...

> offer hospitality to one another without grumbling. Each one should use whatever gift he has received to serve others, faithfully administering God's grace in its various forms. If anyone speaks, he should do it as one speaking the very words of God. If anyone serves, he should do it with the strength God provides, so that in all things God may be praised through Jesus Christ (NIV).

Did you notice the phrase "If anyone serves, he should do it with the strength God provides"? This gives us hope and strength when we have to step outside our comfort zone to be a blessing to others. I find great joy in knowing there is a divine source of help in those situations. When I don't know exactly what to say or how to act in the presence of someone's grief, I lean on the Lord for wisdom.

Thankfully, the passage also recognizes that each person does indeed possess a unique strength in the area of hospitality. In the instances where I have come face-to-face with another's tragedy, I know I am at liberty to minister God's love to them in the way God has designed me to do so. That is, through my actions. God uses some of us to *say*, He uses others of us to *do*. The question then becomes, Where do I fit in? I sincerely believe I am in the latter category.

A good example of someone who used her gift of hospitality that didn't include many words comes from a lady in Virginia. Molly was a young woman with a seemingly perfect life. She had a wonderful, hard-working husband, John, and a sweet-as-pie, three-year-old son, Timmy. One beautiful Saturday morning Molly was running errands and John and Timmy were on their way to the park for some father–son bonding time. It wasn't until that afternoon that Molly got the call that devastated her. Her husband and son had been killed in a car accident on the way home from the park. In the blink of an eye she lost the two most important relationships in her life. A good friend of hers, knowing that the first few days would be the most difficult, decided to stay a couple of days with her dear friend. Jenny was not only there during the day to comfort Molly, but she literally held her friend through the dark, lonely nights as Molly wept and dealt with the heaviness of severe loss. Jenny didn't say much; her actions ministered to Molly.

Another tender example of how meaningful and timely quiet love can be is shown by the actions of my good friend Deanna. Her work as a pediatrician requires her to sometimes witness families in the process of losing a child in the hospital. She says that in those settings she rarely says a word. She just sits in the corner of the patient's room while the family waits for the tragic end to their loved one's short life. Although it may seem she's just sitting there, actually she's praying for the family and their loved one. The family can't hear her prayers, but they can sense them, and they are aware of her comforting presence as they say their last goodbyes.

A woman from Georgia told me that when she and her husband were out of town for the funeral of her father, a couple from their church went to their home, planted flowers, and worked on the landscaping. When Tammy and her husband got home they were astounded. Not only were there flowers, but the lawn had been mowed and new mulch had been put down. What a welcomed treat. Sometimes actions effectively show the love of God.

The following ideas might come in handy the next time you want to *do* love rather than *say* love. These suggestions were given by women who answered a questionnaire question:

> *If you have ever lost a loved one through death, what was the most meaningful thing someone did for you to show their sympathy and love?* [I've added some additional thoughts in brackets.]

- I was grateful for the flowers that were sent. [Make sure the flowers don't require special care.]

- Our neighbors brought meals to our family. It was such a relief not to have to cook during such a trying time. [If possible find out if someone is coordinating providing meals.]

- The most meaningful things after the death of my mother were the handwritten notes that were sent following the funeral. [Sending a handwritten note acknowledging the pain a friend is going through really uplifts and encourages someone who is grieving.]

- I was consumed by the sadness of losing my sister and was unable to talk to every visitor at the wake. I did notice their presence. I regretted that I couldn't speak to each one, but after the service, in the quiet of my memory of the day, I recalled the friendly faces who made the effort to be there. It was a sincere blessing to know they cared. I hope someday to tell each one how much I appreciated their thoughtfulness. [Just being present at a funeral and giving a hug can bless someone more than we realize.]

Giving Comfort Through Words

While some of us are gifted at showing God's love, others are gifted with the ability to say the right thing at the right time. I deeply admire those who have and use this precious gift. I think of a woman in Florida who told me that at her mother's funeral a young lady came up and told her that her mother had handmade her prom dress. The daughter didn't know her mother had done such a sweet thing for that young lady. What a blessing it was for her to hear what her mother had done and be reminded of her love.

If you don't know what to say, do something to show how you feel. You've been given an opportunity to show God's love and peace to someone who needs it. Take it!

The young lady who was willing to share such a warm memory is to be commended for being such a worthy vessel of appropriate words. Essentially what she did was follow the wisdom in Proverbs 25:11: "Like apples of gold in settings of silver is a word spoken in right circumstances." The grieving daughter's response is evidence that when words are from heaven they can heal. Which leads to a sobering fact that if they are not "anointed" words, they can potentially be hurtful to the hearer, even if they're said with good intentions. For this reason, it is important to weigh carefully what we say. First Peter 4:11 advises, "If anyone speaks, he should do it as one speaking the very words of God."

Unfortunately, I can remember a time when my own words were not fitly spoken. My mother's dearly loved aunt had passed away, and I immaturely responded. As my mother and her sisters were wiping the tears and consoling each other I spoke up and said, "Hey—she's in heaven now. Why be sad?" As a young teenager I obviously didn't exercise the best discernment or discretion in the moment. My comment was my way of trying to lift my mother's spirit. Her reaction, however, is something I will never forget. She tenderly said, "I know you're trying to make me feel better, but right now I just need to grieve."

When ministering to those who are mourning the loss of a loved one, make sure you correctly and wisely use the gift God has given you. Doing nothing can be just as painful as saying or doing the wrong thing. I have a friend who suffered a miscarriage before I knew her, and she said that most of her friends didn't mention the loss. All she wanted to hear was an "I'm sorry." But they didn't understand or know what to do. She finally had to go to them and ask them to acknowledge her pain. If you don't know what to say, do something to show how you feel. You've been given an opportunity to show God's love and peace to someone who needs it. Take it!

The New Arrival

On a lighter note, the arrival of a newborn is a great opportunity to offer support and love. Sometimes we're not aware how much a new mom can use some tender loving care.

Having gotten the "I'm a new mom" T-shirt I can say from experience that there are some very nice things that can be done to bless a woman who is close to giving birth or has just given birth. Here are a few that really made a difference and spoke love to me.

- *Offer to keep the older children while the pregnant mom is in the hospital giving birth.* Let the parents know you're available anytime day or night to take on this responsibility. If it's late, volunteer to pick up the kids or stay at their house until morning.

- *Host a baby shower.* If this will be the mom's first child, plan a classic baby shower for close friends and family. If this is the second or third, ask guests to bring gift cards. The mom probably has baby equipment such as a crib, stroller, and car seat. What she most likely will need are little things, such as new bottles, pacifiers, and baby clothes. Another good idea is to ask the mom to provide a wish list or register at a reasonably priced store (this can even be done online now!).

- *The small, mundane chores moms do before they're nine months pregnant or right after giving birth can seem monumental. Offer to do some grocery shopping, pick up dry cleaning, pick up stamps, or anything else she needs.* After offering, say, "We can settle up on the cost when I get back" so there are no misunderstandings. Running errands will bless the new parent(s) and give them more time to spend with their new bundle of hard work...er...I mean joy.

- *Organize a meal chain.* The people in my church brought meals to Emmitt and me on Tuesdays and Thursdays for the first two months of our daughter's life. What a blessing to not have to think about what to cook for dinner on those nights. It also gave each of our friends a chance for a quick visit to meet our new family member.

- One of the hardest things for a mom-to-be and a new mom is housework. *Offer to help clean the home,* especially during the last trimester when normal tasks become daunting challenges. The nearly impossible task of leaning over to clean a toilet is the last challenge a fully pregnant mom wants to face.

- *If the mom already has children, offer to take them for a day so the soon-to-be-mom or new mom and dad can get some one-on-one time with her new baby...*or even have peace and quiet while the baby is sleeping. Arrange a special outing to a zoo or a movie to let the older kids know they are special too.

While it is undeniably rewarding to bless a new mother and father with gifts and actions, there are some clear guidelines for what to do and what not to do.

Unless asked to do so, don't show up in the delivery room with a film crew behind you—or even a hand-held camcorder. Not every mom wants her "double chin push" documented, and not every mom wants an audience to see a close-up of her red, sweat-drenched face while she's pushing a seven-pound human being out of her body.

Visiting a new mom and child in the hospital is a very kind and loving thing to do, but there are caveats.

Another bad idea is to assume the birth mother would like company in the delivery room besides her mate and the attending doctors and nurses. A good friend of mine told me that when she was in the hospital having her first child a coworker walked into the delivery room to visit with her while she was in early labor. At first my friend was flattered that this sweet, yet somewhat inappropriate visit was taking place. She thought it was just a quick pass-through until her "guest" sat down in a chair beside her hospital bed. She took out her knitting needles and went to work on a sweater. "It's so nice that the doctors told me anyone could be in the delivery room while you're having your baby!" she said. "I can't wait to watch. I have enough yarn to last me all night!"

Needless to say my friend was shocked and in the awkward position of telling this friend she couldn't stay. So unless specifically invited by the mom—don't show up.

Visiting a new mom and child in the hospital is a very kind and loving thing to do, but there are caveats for that too.

- *The delivery room is invitation only.* And it doesn't matter if 30 years ago you were the one who pushed the soon-to-be new mom out of your body.

- *Call ahead before visiting.* Impromptu visits can be awkward and sometimes embarrassing for the new mom.

- *Never bring a sick child to the delivery or recovery rooms.* Wait till the child is 100 percent better before visiting the new mom and baby.

- *Ask to hold the newborn. And always wash your hands before touching the child.* In fact, that should be the very first thing you do when arriving in the maternity ward.

- *If bringing a gift, make sure it can be easily transported.* Gifts such as strollers and jungle gyms can be mentioned, but deliver them to the mom's home.

A house visit, instead of a hospital visit, is more than likely what most moms prefer. There are guidelines for this kind of visit as well. Some of them are the same as hospital visits, such as calling ahead, never bringing a sick child, and washing your hands. However, there are a few new ideas to consider.

- *Never ring the doorbell.* There is a good chance the infant is sleeping and ringing a loud doorbell could interrupt precious sleep (the mom's especially). A soft knock on the door should do the trick if the mom isn't sleeping.

- *Bring a meal or a pack of diapers or both.* It's good to not arrive empty-handed. The new parents can use all the help they can get.

- *Don't stay too long.* A lengthy, drawn-out visit is tiring for sleep-deprived parents.

One humorous story about a mother who preferred to be visited at home involves my best friend who told me a few weeks before her delivery that she didn't want any visitors in the hospital. I respected that wish and didn't make a trip to see her until she was home. Admittedly, I had assumed that a visit from *me*, her closest friend, would be welcome and that I would be *the* exception, but that wasn't the case. It took everything within me to respect her wish, but I'm glad I did.

I found out later that her baby came sooner than expected, and she didn't have a chance to e-mail everyone with her request for no visitors. She ended up having 50 or so people come to the hospital.

Don't Forget Dad

The nine months of pregnancy, birth of a new life, and the following months are such special times for the new mother and father. Unfortunately, the father is often forgotten when it comes to helping out. Remember, he's in for some sleepless nights and dirty diapers too. What can we do to help new dads? Try these.

- *Bring food to the hospital for the hungry but proud-as-can-be father.* When I was recovering in the hospital after my C-section, my meals were provided by the hospital, but Emmitt was on his own. He tried to make it to the hospital cafeteria when he could, but being an attentive new father and husband, he didn't make it there very often. If it weren't for our mothers bringing him food, he'd be a lot skinnier now!

- *Arrange to sit with the new mom* in the hospital or at home so the dad can get out and run errands or have some personal time.

- *Offer to spend the night and help the new mom with nighttime feedings so the new dad can get a full-night's sleep.* This is especially important if the new dad doesn't have very much time off from work. My mom and mother-in-law did this for Emmitt, and he greatly appreciated it.

Gift Ideas for New Parents

One of my favorite things about pregnancy and births are the gifts. Not just receiving them (Ok, I admit…I love getting presents. Who doesn't, really?), but I love giving gifts even more. Whether I'm attending a baby shower or taking a gift to a home visit, there is nothing like the joy of giving to make the day brighter. Here are some gift-giving ideas to show you love, care, and support the mom, dad, older siblings, and newborn.

- When I was recovering in the hospital my sister-in-law and best friend, Stephanie, brought in a fragrance diffuser. She knew I love scented candles, but being in a hospital it probably wasn't a good idea to have an open flame. The diffuser made the room smell pretty and, at the same time, kept the hospital safe from destruction. What a great and practical gift.

- My husband's office sent a gift basket filled with snacks for Emmitt and magazines for me. Instead of sending the typical flowers, which I also love, they sent something both Emmitt and I needed—food and entertainment.

- Gift cards make great gifts. You can get these cards from grocery stores, department stores, and supermarkets. You can also make your own gift certificates for the new family, for activities such as helping arrange a date night for the parents and watching their kids, a housecleaning certificate, or a trip to the zoo for the older siblings. Be creative!

- For the baby, purchase clothes that are sized for 6- to 9-month-olds and diapers that are two to three sizes bigger than the baby is wearing at the moment. That way he or she has clothes to wear while growing and the parents will be helped when the new baby gifts stop coming in.

- Siblings who are only slightly older might have a lot of adjusting to do when the new brother or sister arrives. Help make the transition easier by taking small gifts to them when you take a new baby present. This will help them to feel included and not forgotten.

A Delightful Post-Birth Kindness

One of the most hospitable things ever done for me after giving birth is something I hope to do for others. When my husband and I brought our first daughter, Lily, home from the hospital, my dear mother-in-law met us at the door. She'd been staying in our home while I was recovering in the hospital after my C-section. Emmitt and I were exhausted, a little scared, and a bit anxious about all the changes and the new little one in our lives. When we pulled into the driveway, there was Tish. She was a beautiful sight to see! When I walked into my home I couldn't believe my eyes. Everything was sparkling clean, there were candles lit, soft music was playing, and the comforter and sheets on my bed were pulled down, waiting for me to crawl in. What a welcome! I will never forget her hospitality. I was definitely in need of a blessing.

Others Need Us Too

Showing hospitality isn't limited to being available when death calls or when new life begins. There are many other life situations when people need love and attention. When someone arrives home after surgery, depending on the type of procedure done, there can be a long recovery time. A woman in Kentucky told me that when she was home recovering from surgery a friend came to her house one morning and took her children for the entire day. When evening came she brought the children back, bathed them, and put them to bed. The convalescing mom felt as if she had died and gone to heaven! Her friend went above and beyond the call of duty and ministered to that mother (and the kids!) greatly.

If you want to show hospitality, why not do these?

- *Take meals.* A woman told me that when she was home recovering from major surgery for six weeks various friends from church brought her and her husband meals. The hot meals brought them great comfort.

- *Run errands for the patient.* Offer to make a run to the grocery store or the bank or anywhere she or he would normally need to go. Also offer to take children to and from school or to activities.

- *Do household chores.* What better way to show someone you care than to be up to your elbows in their dirty dishes!

- *Take care of outside chores.* Mowing the lawn or watering flowers is a great way to help out.

- *Do anything she or he might need.* Remember, if you tell someone to "call me for anything," make sure you're willing to follow through (within reason).

Disaster Relief

Have you known someone who lost everything they own in a house fire? Or whose home was destroyed due to a natural disaster? There are so many victims today due to uncontrollable circumstances. Lately it seems like more natural disasters are occurring and ravaging a lot of neighborhoods. Hurricane Katrina is the first to come to mind. When I heard about what happened I felt so helpless. I couldn't go there to help clean up the mess, but I did what I could. I took a trip to a wholesale warehouse and purchased cases of diapers, formula, and wipes. I dropped them off at a local church that was filling a tractor-trailer full of donations to take to the mothers and fathers and children who were in dire need. And more disasters will surely follow. Tornadoes, earthquakes, and tsunamis seem to be everywhere.

A friend of mine had a coworker named Beth whose rented home was demolished by fire. Beth was out of town at the time, and all she had left were the clothes in her small overnight bag. The company she worked for decided to take up donations for the fire victim. There were financial and material contributions made so that she could restart her life with more than the clothes on her back. She was also given a temporary place to stay with my friend until she could find an apartment. Beth told her new roommate that never in her life had she been shown more kindness or love. Even though she'd lost everything, she felt like she had gained something priceless—the awareness that God was looking out for her through His people. What a blessing!

Here are some other ways to help someone who has lost everything:

- *Financial donations.* Make sure you know where your money is going. It was shameful how many fake charities were started after Katrina. There are horrible human beings who will use a tragedy to fill their own pocketbooks.

- *Material donations.* Find out what is most needed and donate those items. Food, water, diapers, formula, and other life-sustaining and durable items are always needed.

- *Sweat donations.* Going to the site of tragedy and helping people rebuild what was destroyed is a very good way to show you care.

"Offer hospitality" (1 Peter 4:9 NIV). Have you considered that these words aren't merely a suggestion? They are a command, one that many of us may obey and not even realize it. When my father-in-law left the note next to the coffeemaker on that July morning that said "Just push the button," he might not have known that he was following a biblical directive. When the woman held the grieving widow all night long, whether she knew it or not, hers were the arms of God's love. When the coworker opened her apartment to her friend whose house burned, maybe she wasn't aware her actions were speaking God's tender care.

We are surrounded every day by people who are in dire straits and may feel paralyzed by life's circumstances. When we see a need and step in to help that person, God takes note of our contributions and can use them to bring help and healing. Consider the man in Mark 2 who was paralyzed physically. Four friends carried him to the house where Christ was teaching. They couldn't get to the Lord because of the crowd so, in desperation, they removed the roof and lowered the paralytic into the room. Isn't this a beautiful description of what happens when friends help friends? Jesus saw their faith and told the paralyzed man his sins were forgiven. A little later He told the man to pick up his mat and go home. Many times the faith of friends makes a huge difference.

15

To Do or Not to Do

One of the hazards of being hospitable is the inevitable encounter with a guest who can try the patience of the most gracious of hosts. Having a run-in with a visitor who tests your steel is a "not if, but when" situation. My (Annie) sweet husband has been through enough of the "I can't wait till they leave" tragedies through the years to motivate him to create some new words to describe the dilemma:

- *"Hostiletality"*—The act of maiming a guest who is being obnoxious.

- *"Hospitaltality"*—The facility where an obnoxious guest who has been maimed is taken.

- *"Hospicetality"*—A place where maimed guests go for ongoing treatment of injuries received from exasperated host.

- *"Hospifatality"*—The extreme version of "hostiletality."

The expected approach to offering do's and don'ts is to suggest ways you can maintain a heavenly attitude while the annoying person is in your home. However, let's look at some tips to keep *us* from becoming tagged (especially on the toe) as an unwanted guest.

To help those of us who want to never be put on the list of "Oh no—not them!" guests, the following wisdom gathered through a nonformal survey will help us be better hosts *and* terrific guests.

Being Content with What They Have

Traveling with our family of four over the past 30 or so years has yielded countless opportunities to experience hospitality in many forms. One particular trip to the Southwest clearly demonstrated the extremes. The church where we were to present a concert in Texas graciously offered to make arrangements for our housing for the duration of our stay. Imagine our sheer delight when we realized that our housing would be in a beautiful, spacious mansion. My eyes captured the finery and exquisite beauty of this lovely home. The rooms seemed to go on forever. We had never stayed in such an impressive dwelling. This was going to be a weekend we would never forget. The host and hostess were so loving and gracious. We left feeling like we'd been staying at a five-star resort and had made lifelong friends.

Only when love fills a house will it be an inviting
place where family and guests feel totally welcome
and want to return again and again.

Reluctantly we left the gated community and all the affluence that it represented. We made our way to the next event. Heading west we arrived at our destination rested and excited about the coming day. Gratefully, the church where we were to minister also provided housing during our stay. However, this time it was not in a gated community within a 10,000-square-foot mansion. No, we were given a tiny little trailer with barely enough room for us to turn around. I remember that when we ate our breakfast the next morning, the couple hosting us stood, holding their plates in their hands because there wasn't enough chairs or room around the table for us all to sit at the same time.

When it came to housing arrangements, the contrast couldn't have been more stark. But we felt as welcomed and cared for in the little trailer as we did in the opulent palace. The square footage, or the lack thereof, was never a concern. The warm feelings of hospitality that were freely lavished upon us were the same. Each hosting couple generously gave to us their very best, and each loving gesture was more than sufficient.

What a gift from God that these two experiences happened so close together! It was so important for our kids to see that the differences, though extreme, didn't matter one bit. And it was a great reminder for Steve and me too. It was that weekend, in fact, that our little family adopted a family motto that originated with the apostle Paul but with a little twist: "We're content in whatever state *they* are in."

Regardless of how wonderful our houses may be, "unless the LORD builds the house, they labor in vain who build it" (Psalm 127:1). So much attention these days is given to bricks-and-mortar construction, exquisite interior decorating, and lavish furnishings. Only when love fills a house will it be an inviting place where family and guests feel totally welcome and want to return again and again.

Staying Overnight

The following "not to do" as guests are not exhaustive, but they represent some challenges hosts face.

- *Don't wash your makeup off or clean your shoes with your host's washcloths.* Often these are linens only brought out when there is overnight company and the host wants to keep them nice. If you don't see any older cloths, ask for one.

- *Don't leave personal items out.* If the bathroom is shared, don't leave personal items or clothes there. Take them back to your room.

- *Don't stay up after your host has gone to bed.* Be sensitive to the fact that while you, as the guest, may have a flexible schedule and be able to sleep in, others in the household may have to be up early and go to work. If you want to stay up all night and watch television, rent a motel room and visit your friends.

- *Don't invite yourself to stay with someone you don't know* (i.e., a friend of a friend) for the sole purpose of avoiding the cost of a hotel room. Housing and feeding people costs the host money, effort, and time.

One lady who is a veritable hospitality magnet and regularly finds herself housing missionaries, evangelists, folks attending conventions, or those who just need a place to stay, offered this insight:

> The Lord has blessed us so much, and we seek to share that blessing with others. I don't mind if people come and stay with us because they can't afford a hotel room. In fact, we've had people stay with us for days, weeks, months, and even years during our married life. Most of the time it works out fine for all of us. We've been privileged to meet some of God's great warriors and have often benefited more from their presence than they have from our hospitality. Of course, there have been a few incidences where we've felt used and abused. Those situations were not fun. I understand there will always be folks who will take advantage and mistreat those who are trying to help. But I'm willing to deal with the few "bad apples" who might exploit our good graces in order to help those who really need it. No one said that following Christ would be a cakewalk.

Now, back to some tips to being a good guest.

- *Don't be disrespectful.* Abide by or be sensitive to your host's moral, religious, and social convictions. When in doubt, don't ask. Err on the conservative side. Whether the policy is no smoking, no drinking, no drugging, or no cohabiting of unmarried couples, follow the wishes of the host.

- *Do make your bed each morning.* Tidy up the bed even if you close the door to the room you're using.

- *Don't leave wet towels or clothes on the floor.*

- *Do use a napkin or coaster when placing a glass or cup on the furniture.* You want your host to remember your visit because it was so enjoyable, not because you ruined her great-grandmother's coffee table.

- *Avoid controversial issues, making statements you know are opposite the opinions of your host, or bringing up family issues that will dredge up hard feelings.* There is plenty to discuss without stirring up an argument or opening old wounds.

- *Never complain about the food being served.* If you have a food allergy or health concern that has a direct bearing on what you can and should eat, send a written note to your host *well in advance* of your visit. Most hosts want to accommodate your needs. A quick e-mail or short letter can help avoid an embarrassing situation. If you have a child who is a finicky eater, bring food you know your child will eat (teach your child not to complain or make comments about what is served) or send a list of foods you know your child will be comfortable eating. Be specific about brands.

- *Never leave evidence of intimate "good times."*

- *Don't be late.* If you're detained for any reason, give your host a call with an updated time of arrival.

- *Don't use the TV or sound equipment until you check with the host.* You don't want to mess up his or her system. If you have children with you, don't allow them to turn on electronics until the host has fully explained how they operate. A suggestion for hosting: Photocopy the remote control. With arrows and written directions, note how to operate the apparatus, laminate the instructions, and leave them beside the entertainment equipment.)

- *Don't feed the family pet from your dinner plate or even scraps after dinner without permission.*

- *Keep remarks about the decorating style or furnishings positive.*

Be sensitive to comments that might be construed as criticism.

- *Don't take a tour of the house without permission from the host. And don't ask for a tour of the house.* It's not your decision to wander the premises. *And if a door is closed, don't go in.*

- *Don't use your host's computer unless the host invites you or says you can.* If you are offered the use of their computer, keep your time to a minimum. And if you need to print documents, such as an e-mail or airline boarding pass, ask for permission. Also, never let your children surf the web on a guest's computer without asking for permission.

- *Don't do laundry unless the host offers you this courtesy.* If there is an emergency regarding your clothes, politely ask if you can use the washing machine and dryer.

- *Don't use the telephone land line for long-distance calls unless the host suggests it.*

- *Ask where the bathroom is.* Your host may not want you opening closet doors trying to find it.

- *Don't allow children to run through the house, take food from the kitchen, rough-play with pets, or handle decorative items.* No matter how ill-behaved your children may be at home, keep control of them while you're visiting others. If this isn't possible, have them stay elsewhere.

- *If you know your car has a serious oil or transmission fluid leak, ask for a shield (cardboard, for example) for the fluid to drip on or where you should park.*

- *Never bring an animal of any kind or size along unless it is encouraged by the host.* If your host knows you have a pet, let him or her extend the invitation to your furry critter. Don't put your host in the position of feeling pressured to say yes to you bringing your creature. (I owe my in-laws a big apology.

We've been guilty of bringing along Bob, our dog; Tilly, our cockatiel; and Jenkins, our chicken the kids got at Easter. We even took a fish I hoped wouldn't survive the trip. Now I know better. Sorry, Lillian and P.J.!)

- *Never light a cigarette or cigar inside the host's home.* Always assume you are to go outside and smoke. Don't throw cigarette or cigar butts on the ground.

- *Never look in the refrigerator or pantry without a specific invitation by the hosts.* Don't help yourself or make yourself at home unless you're asked to.

- *Do ask before turning on the television and also ask what program people want to watch.* Remember, you are there to visit with the hosts (usually), not entertain yourself.

- *Don't fall asleep on the couch.* If you're really tired and need to rest, ask if you can lie down on a bed.

- *Never try to take over and instruct the host on how to do something better.* Stay in your place as the guest.

- *Keep the furniture and other items where they are.* Also, never check for dust bunnies unless it's Easter.

- *Do use good table manners.* Don't shove your food onto your fork with your fingers. Don't reach across the table. Ask if you need something that is out of reach. All the good manners your mother tried to teach you when you were a kid are somewhere in the back of your mind. Before you go for a visit, find them, dust them off, and take them with you.

- *Don't scold or correct the host's children.* If you think the children are disruptive, stay in a motel.

- *Take refreshments when offered.* If your host insists you take along a snack or leftovers, do it with a grateful attitude. Even if you don't plan on eating the food, be polite and accept the gesture of hospitality.

- *Never ask to take food home with you.* If your host suggests it, then you may graciously accept.

- *Don't blow your nose at the table or pick your teeth in the presence of others.* Go to the restroom.

- *Don't leave the commode lid up.* Don't fail to flush.

- *Never be the one to suggest that you spend the night.* That should be the decision and suggestion of the host.

- *Stay positive about the accommodations.* Be grateful you have a place to sleep. If you can't be appreciative or you are terribly uncomfortable, go to a motel. Don't make your host feel like his or her best is not good enough.

- *Don't strip your bed before you leave unless asked to.* Sometimes pillows and mattress pads are freshly laundered but have stains and don't look very good.

- *Don't come to visit if you're sick.* One woman recounted that when she was a child a family came to visit and one of the children had been newly diagnosed with polio. As much as they loved that family, they didn't want to be exposed to something that dangerous. The woman's mother immediately took her kids to the doctor and had them vaccinated. Be very careful, even if the ailment is a simple cold.

Good Guests...

- *Good guests always offer to help in any way they can.* Perhaps they can help to set the table or clear the table.

- *Good guests offer to take off their shoes if it is snowy, raining, or muddy outside.* Showing you care about the host and her house is always a good idea.

- *Good guests will be sensitive to the needs of the host.* Is the baby crying? Offer to pick up the child. Do the potatoes need to be peeled? Ask for a knife and a bowl. Does the dog need to be walked? Offer to take the dog out.

- *Good guests arrive on time and in good moods.*

- *Really good guests leave on time.*

- *Good guests bring a host gift, such as a candle, personalized stationery, a special food item, and/or a surprise for the children.*

- *Good guests send or leave a written thank-you note.*

- *Good guests keep their space clean and orderly.* And upon their departure, they leave their room as clean or cleaner than they found it. If you don't want to tidy up, stay in a motel.

- *Good guests follow the host's routine.* When the host or hostess retire to their room, follow their lead and go to bed.

- *Good guests show their gratitude.* Say "Thank you!" "May I help you?" "We had a lovely time!"

- *Good guests control their children.*

- *Good guests don't expect to be waited on.* They find ways to serve.

- *Good guests are quick to compliment.* If you enjoyed a dish, ask for the recipe.

- *Good guests know good manners—and use them.*

A Few Do's and Don'ts for Hosts

Just as it is the responsibility of the guest to make sure all plans are well understood, this is doubly important for the host to make sure all arrangements are clear. Putting your plans and expectations in writing will help alleviate the possibility of a misunderstanding or at least minimize the risk of miscommunication. I find this letter pretty straightforward.

Dear Loved One,
    I'm so glad you and your husband are able to come for the weekend of November 20. Steve and I are looking forward

to it and expecting you to stay with us at our house. (Or, if you prefer, you might say, "I'm enclosing the number and e-mail address for a couple of really great hotels that aren't far from our house. From what I've heard you should be very comfortable there.")

Do you or your husband have any special dietary needs I should be aware of? I want to prepare foods you both will be able to eat.

I can hardly wait to catch up with all that's been happening in your world since we last visited. A couple of our friends will be joining us for dinner on Friday evening around six o'clock. I believe you'll enjoy getting to know them. When do you expect to arrive on Friday? If six is too early for you, just let me know. We are very flexible on this end.

You have several options for Saturday afternoon. I can offer you some suggestions of fun things to do or link you to some websites that offer local activities for that weekend. If you would like some company on your outing, Steve and I would be happy to show you the sights. Did you have anything special in mind that you particularly wanted to do or see? Or, if you'd rather, we can just kick back and relax here at home. I'm planning a casual cookout for Saturday evening dinner. Our children will be joining us. They really wanted to see you while you were here.

I was wondering what your plans are for Sunday? If your schedule permits it, we would love to take you to church with us and then come back to our house for lunch before you leave. How does that sound? If you have other plans and need to leave earlier, we can have either a quick continental breakfast or a more relaxing meal before you go. I really want to accommodate your schedule.

We are so grateful you're taking the time and making the effort to come to see us. We really want you to enjoy your time with us and have a relaxing visit.

A simple letter such as this covers many, if not all, the questions you need answered: time of arrival, lodging expectations, dietary needs, free time expectations, and time of departure.

Here are some additional suggestions to make your guests' visits more enjoyable.

- *If your guests have small children, do your best to prepare for their needs.* See if you can borrow items such as a playpen, portable crib, high chair, stroller, and a few toys. Be sure to tell them ahead of time exactly what you have for the child to use. If you borrow these items, make sure they are clean and in good repair.

- *Don't complain about all the things you didn't get done* in preparing for your guests' arrival. That makes them feel like they are imposing and are not welcome in your home.

- *Don't make comments that compare your house to theirs,* such as, "Your house is much nicer than ours. Our home is not nearly as big and beautiful as yours." Such comments not only show an ungrateful attitude on your part for the home God has given you, but it also puts your guest in an uncomfortable position of trying to refute your statement. Keep the atmosphere fun and relaxed.

- *Stay out of the rooms you've assigned to your guests* during their visit unless first checking with them or letting them know the room will be used during the day. Request that any wet towels or clothes that need to be laundered be brought to the laundry room or left outside the bedroom door.

- If you haven't slept in your guest room lately you may be unaware of items that are missing. *Check and see if the mattress is comfortable, and if there are adequate blankets and pillows.* Make sure there is a large or full-length mirror. Supply a clock/radio and a place to set their suitcases. Make sure there is room in the closet for your guests to hang clothes. Pay attention to the lighting in the room. You may need a stronger light bulb. Is the temperature stuffy? Perhaps a floor fan or ceiling fan would make the room more comfortable. Consider providing a comfortable bathrobe, some interesting reading material, and a chair. A basket with snack foods and bottled water adds a welcoming atmosphere.

Becoming a Gracious Host

- *Start small.* Invite one couple over for dessert before you plan a dinner party for 12.

- *Maintain a teachable spirit* and borrow ideas from those who entertain well. It's amazing how much we can learn by observing others, reading decorating/entertaining magazines, and asking questions of those who do it right.

- *Go ahead and extend the invitation to that couple you've had on your heart.* After you've committed to having them over, you will rise to the occasion.

- *Ask for help.* Perhaps your first big dinner party should be a potluck. Have two or three couples over. Assign one to bring a salad, another to bring a vegetable, and one to bring a dessert. You can be in charge of the meat, bread, and drinks. This is a great way to have a nice dinner party without taking on more than you can handle.

- *Make your guests feel special* by asking them to tell you their life stories. When you make the conversation about them, they are sure to enjoy the visit. *Caution:* Be prepared for interesting responses.

- *Provide a relaxed atmosphere* by being ready ahead of time. I try to be completely dressed and ready an hour before my guests arrive. I finish any work that needs to be done wearing an apron. When you avoid running around at the last minute like a hysterical chicken, you'll enjoy your company more.

- *Prepare the guest room with the touches of a gracious host.*

Providing flowers, candy, bottled water, and bathrobes can make a visit extra special for your guests. Also provide some beautiful, relaxing music (Heidi's CD "Hymns from God's Great Cathedral" is a great choice for your guest room) along with an easy-to-operate CD player.

Our dear friend Kay DeKalb Smith is a traveling speaker/singer/comedian. She's stayed in homes across the country. She shared with me one particular visit that she will never forget. Kay had been traveling extensively and was unbelievably exhausted. During the week, she was scheduled to stay in the home of a friend. Her host put her in a bedroom that was filled with everything she could possibly need. It was located at the end of the hallway, far away from all the noise and activity of the rest of the household. When Kay slipped into the bed, she found the most wonderful experience waiting for her. Her friend had received some sheets as a gift with a thread count beyond imagination. Kay later learned her host had taken the sheets off of her own bed, washed and ironed them, and put them on Kay's bed. What an incredible act of love and service this seasoned host showed her guest.

• *Pray for your guests before they arrive and after they leave.* As you clean the room and prepare the amenities that will make their visit comfortable, and as you clean up after their visit, quietly pray for them. This is the best gift you can give.

16

Don't Let Them See You Sweat

Several years ago a maker of deodorant created a commercial that expounded the virtues of its product. To draw the consumer in, the company came up with a catchphrase that became very popular. It said, "Don't let them see you sweat." I (Annie) think of that commercial more often these days now that I'm of "a certain age."

Sweating seems to be a normal part of my day, and it has become about as regular as breathing...and just as involuntary. But I think I've figured out what happened. My thermostat has worn out over so many years, and unfortunately, there seems to be no available replacement part for a model my age. To console myself, I've adopted the attitude I saw on a bumper sticker recently: "I'm not having a hot flash. I'm in the middle of a power surge!" Though these surges are recurring phenomena that I assume (I'm hoping!) will pass in due time, not long ago I had an opportunity to apply the "Don't let them see you sweat" mantra to being hospitable.

My brother and his wife were coming to our house for dinner. Since most of the time I'm the one who makes the 400-mile trip back to see old friends and relatives, this was only their second visit in several years. I was very excited! I invited our children and their families to join us for a big reunion dinner. Since it was only a few weeks before Thanksgiving, I decided a turkey dinner with all the fixin's would be the perfect way to celebrate the long-awaited and much-anticipated visit.

The day of their arrival I got up early to prepare for the evening meal. For some reason I couldn't define, I felt a nudge to start the turkey baking process long before I needed to. I'm not claiming this was due to a supernatural sensitivity, but I do believe God is concerned with the smallest details of His people's days. I followed the nudge and got busy.

Around two o'clock that afternoon my best-laid plans were suddenly changed. As I was putting the finishing touches on the big celebration meal, the unthinkable happened. Suddenly I heard a *huge* explosion outside, and instantly all the power went down. I ran outside to see what happened. Just down the block I saw a huge dump truck with a downed power pole next to it. I learned later that a large transformer had crashed down, throwing sparks everywhere. I guess it was quite spectacular! The wires fell…and electricity stopped.

The wreck sent my carefully crafted schedule up in flames. Along with the cars that had to go around the rubble on the road, my special dinner preparations had to take a detour.

With the electricity down and no hope of getting it restored within a reasonable time, I could feel my sweat glands (not age-related this time!) suddenly fill up and threaten to spill over. That's when the deodorant commercial statement came to me. I decided immediately that I would not let them see me sweat.

Thankfully, the nudge I was now certain had a divine source had gotten me to prepare early, which saved the day. The deviled eggs were safely nestled in their special Tupperware egg-shaped container in the now very quiet, nonfunctioning refrigerator. Dessert was sitting majestically on the cake stand, ready for slicing off a sweet piece of heaven. And the salad was ready, just awaiting a generous splash of salad dressing to top off the job.

With the turkey already fully baked, all I really needed to do was prepare the green beans, mashed potatoes, and rolls. Since my cooktop is fueled by natural gas rather than electricity (a huge advantage in disastrous "no electricity moments"), I knew that cooking the veggies would not be a problem. But what to do about baking the rolls? No one has ever died as a result of not having rolls at a festive dinner, but I was determined to find a way to complete my menu as planned. (I prefer to think of it as perseverance, although some may call it something else.) I quickly went on a mental search through my years of growing up poor in the "hollers" of West Virginia and the very limited power we had. I had to come up with an alternative to using my oven.

Being raised by a resourceful mom who knew how to deal with unforeseen circumstances, I recalled watching her on more than one occasion fry our biscuits instead of bake them when her old, unreliable oven went on the blink. So in the spirit of the "make do" ability my mother exemplified, I took out a frying pan and got the bread process started.

With the food part of the evening well under control, I then thought of another issue…as the fading sunlight began to turn to full darkness. Again looking back in time, I thought of my Grandmother Naomi, who lived her entire life without the luxury of electricity (and without indoor plumbing and running water). Recalling her source of night light, I gathered up a few of the decorative oil lamps on shelves around our home. I carefully filled each ancient-style illuminator with a generous swig of fresh lamp oil, trimmed the wicks, and cleaned the dusty glass chimneys. I felt a real sense of connection to a bygone era as I prepared for an old-time, electricity-free evening, just like pioneers experienced.

Just about the time I'd fully resolved to enjoy…and even revel in… the atmosphere of old times, everything changed again. Thirty minutes before my guests arrived I suddenly heard a hum as the refrigerator motor kicked on. The lights flickered to life, and the music on the FM radio in the kitchen returned, blasting me back to the twenty-first century. As grateful as I was for the restoration of our modern amenities, I was a bit disappointed about not having the unique old-fashioned time I'd changed my plans for. But I wasn't sorry enough to not appreciate returning to all the modern luxuries!

I'm happy to say that I was ready and able to entertain special guests during an unexpected blackout. To be honest, it was a pleasing feeling to know a little inconvenience couldn't sidetrack or upset a festive occasion. How about you? Would you be ready if something unexpected came up in the midst of getting ready for company?

Here are a few tips Heidi and I put together on what to do when challenging situations threaten to heat up your stress level. Our motto? *Keep it simple. Keep on schedule. Keep your focus.*

Keep It Simple

A good way to keep the beads of sweat from forming on our hospitality brows is to be willing to bless our guests with simplicity. One way to do this is to create a menu that is uncomplicated rather than overly involved. This key advice lets us enjoy our company while being ready to give them satisfied tummies. The true essence of hospitality is to make those who enter our doors feel loved by our greeting and the way we've happily prepared for them. If replacing the swanky hors d'oeuvres with a nice, well-arranged plate of cheese and crackers means we're more relaxed and able to engage more with our visitors, then by all means let's go that route. Giving our best to those who enter our doors doesn't always have to mean fancy, elaborate, or expensive.

This approach can also extend to simplifying the table setting. A friend of mine often serves meals on paper plates and provides plasticware. She feels that a quick-and-easy cleanup leaves more time for a fun game of charades or lively conversation. I (Annie) will say her tables are never dull or predictable. Even with the throwaway plates and utensils, she presents very colorful and interesting place settings. At one party celebrating people turning 50 she had black tablecloths, zebra-striped plates, and other festive touches. Every party has a theme. Simple doesn't mean boring. Plastic, disposable plates that look like china as well as plastic utensils that look like silverware are available at nearly all department and discount stores. How terrific! The look of elegance and none of the cleanup...and not a drop of sweat.)

Keep on Schedule

One of the best ways to avoid the unexpected sweat-box of hospitality is to prepare ahead of time. An old adage says that hosting an event is 90 percent mental and 50 percent physical. You may think this is a bit off, but truth be told, it represents the fact that entertaining guests often demands much more than we anticipate. Because of the potential for unexpected interruptions or disruptions, establishing and keeping a schedule is often critical to trouble-free occasions.

When we keep on a schedule, by the time our guests
arrive we'll be rested, ready, and responsive.

When hosting a dinner party, why not set the table the day before (if it's doable and practical considering your circumstances)? I place the serving dishes on the table with notes next to each one noting what food will be served in them. This helps me with the placement of the dishes and reminds me of what I'm planning on serving and if there's any last-minute details I need to consider. (More than once I've opened the refrigerator after a meal to discover I forgot to put out some gelatin or a fruit plate. I'm sure you can relate.)

I use a yellow legal pad to note my entertaining schedule and keep it on track. Each day I list the tasks that need to be accomplished. There is a real sense of triumph when I take my pencil and cross items off the list. (I learned something very helpful from my sister, Gayle, about "to do" lists that I've adopted. When she finds and does a job not on her list, she writes it down and then immediately draws a line through it. She says it raises her feeling of accomplishment plus helps her remember to add it to the list next time. And she's right!)

When we keep on schedule, by the time our guests arrive we'll be ready, rested, and responsive. I even schedule getting bathed, dressed, and prettied-up so I'm ready at least an hour before the arrival of my guests. If you decide to incorporate this idea into your schedule, make sure you wear a clean, beautiful apron to protect your clothes in case any last-minute preparations come up.

When creating a schedule, there are some things you can do to make the festive occasion happen more smoothly and with less stress.

- Clean and purge the house days in advance. Schedule the bulk of housework so it's done long before your guests arrive. This way any last-minute cleanup takes less effort.

- Cook, bake, and freeze as many dishes in advance as possible. If you have your menu planned ahead of time, you'll have a lot less work to be done while your guests are looking on. (Pay close attention to what is in the middle of the table. If you have the main course planned and prepared, the side dishes are a much easier job.)

- Avoid taking on major projects (painting, wallpapering, renovating, refinishing) at least a week before your company arrives. When you take on a huge project you can count on three things: 1) It will take longer than you thought, 2) it will cost more than you planned, and 3) it will be much messier than you anticipated. So to avoid the panicked, perspiration-filled situation that occurs when you are caught running out of time, patience, and money, schedule such jobs well ahead of your event.

Keep Your Focus

When the dump truck went off the road and caused the electricity to go down around two, I was surprised, and the old sweat glands started pumping. It was only after a quick realignment of attitudes that I was able to get my sights back on my priorities. The focus of hospitality should always be on the people you are hosting.

What would have happened if I hadn't put the turkey in the oven five hours before I'd originally planned? Would the world have come to an end if I served my company Chinese take-out or had to call the local pizza delivery guy? Of course not. The focus of the evening wasn't the stuffed bird, mashed potatoes, and gravy. The reason for the evening was reconnecting with family. Maintaining the primary focus on the reason for the gathering is one of the best ways to not sweat the small stuff.

Successful, Stress-free Entertaining Tips

Unexpected happenings don't have to be as dramatic as a pre-dinner, exploding transformer on a nearby electric pole to test our resolve to not let our guests see us sweat. The mere everydayness of being a host makes some folks wring their hands in worry. But it doesn't have to be that way. Here are a few suggestions that may relieve your stress, help you keep your focus on your guests, and best of all, help your "hospi-brow" stay dry.

- Keep the guest room simple and uncluttered at all times. This way you won't have to scurry to make room for your guest's bags and personal items. Make sure the top of the dresser is clear of trinkets and personal items. Your guest will need a place to put small items.

- If you have only one bathroom, put a medium-to-large mirror in your guest room, preferably over a small dresser so the guests have a place to set makeup and such. It's a small amenity, but it allows your guests more getting-ready time without the need for taking up bathroom time.

- Place a basket of magazines and books by the bed in your guest room. Purchase magazines you think your guests will enjoy and add a cozy throw for comfort.

- Make sure your guest bed has new or very nice pillows. Nobody wants to sleep on old, stained pillows.

- Think of your home as a four-star hotel. Place small chocolates on your guests' pillows or on the nightstand. Place a bottle of water with a glass beside the bed.

- If you don't have a guest-room closet, get a movable wardrobe rack. Your guests need a place to put clothes and overnight bags. Guests also enjoy having their own space.

- Don't hesitate to spoil your guests whenever you can. Heidi had a couple stay overnight in her home who had recently celebrated a wedding anniversary. When they arrived she had a tray of celebratory chocolate-covered strawberries and a bottle of sparkling cider waiting in their room. They were surprised and blessed. Giving visitors an added touch of tender loving care makes them feel special.

- Make sure to have feminine products in the cabinet of your guest bathroom. Women guests will certainly appreciate the thoughtfulness if the need arises.

- If you have the luxury of having two bathrooms, when guests arrive have all family members use one and leave the other for your guests.

- If you're like me, the laundry room and the basement are places you hope no guest ever sees. Put a pleasantly designed notice on the door that says "Private" or "Do Not Enter."

- If your guests are multiday visitors, face the spin-cycle music and anticipate that they'll need to wash and dry clothes. Clean the laundry room and make sure you have an adequate supply of laundry supplies.

- If you're hosting a single event in your home and you don't want guests upstairs, place a velvet or decorative cord across the foot of the stairs.

- If your child's room looks like a disaster area at 6:50 and your guests are arriving at 7:00, simply close the door. Otherwise, take the time to *help* him or her clean up the room.

What About the Kids?

Few things can generate "host sweats" quicker than kids who behave in ways that make guests feel unwelcome or uncomfortable.

Teaching kids how to help visitors feel at ease is a huge undertaking, but here are some basic suggestions.

- Role-play with your kids. Heidi's husband, Emmitt, said his mother used this method with great success. Emmitt's sister, Elizabeth, would be the visitor and he would be the host. She would knock on the door, and Emmitt's mom would invite Elizabeth into the living room and introduce her to Emmitt. He would then stand and welcome her. Then they switched roles. To this day Emmitt and Elizabeth are great hosts.

- Use play dates as teaching tools. I (Heidi) remind Lily that she is the host when her friends come over to play. She knows that as the host she is to share her toys and make her guests feel at home.

- Make a special play date for your child and his or her friends to teach hospitality. Have your child prepare food and get your home ready for the event. Be sure to use kid-friendly recipes. This helps your child understand the importance of showing hospitality to others *and* how much goes into planning and throwing a party.

Here are a few more miscellaneous tips to help keep you cool, calm, and connected to sanity.

- For an emergency cleanup (after the dreaded call that announces "I'll be there in five minutes)," take a large laundry basket and fill it with items lying around the house. Put the basket in a closet or the garage. While you're speed-straightening, heat a pot of scented oil to make the house smell good quickly. It only takes five minutes for the wonderful aroma to fill your house. (If you know your guests have allergies, this isn't a good idea.)

- Keep a bottle of sparkling water or lemonade in your refrigerator and a box of fancy cookies in your pantry for unexpected guests.

- Find a soundtrack of background music you like and keep it near your sound system. You can quickly grab it and have it playing when your surprise guests arrive. It will help them—and you!—relax. I (Heidi) have what I call my "signature sound"— the soundtrack to the movie *Pride and Prejudice*. The classical piano music fills my home with elegance and beauty.

- Have a spare cafeteria-type table that is quickly accessible. If the number of unexpected guests is more than a few, the spare table can be used for a variety of purposes, ranging from a makeshift self-serve drink station to a game table.

- If you're hosting a large party and there are several tables set up, help your guests know where to sit…and make sure everyone has a place. One way to do this is to color coordinate the napkins to your table settings. If a dinner guest takes a green napkin, he or she sits at the table with a green tablecloth in the living room. If someone picks up a white napkin set, he or she sits at the table with the white tablecloth in the dining room. It's a great way of staying organized, and your guests don't have to wander around looking for a place to sit.

Heidi and I have one last tip that is easy to overlook. When guests arrive, we need to put aside all the rushing around we've done and enjoy their presence. If we go on and on about all the work we did or all the things we didn't get done, our guests may feel they've inconvenienced us or that we're frustrated they've arrived. And yes, we did get ready for them and we did put effort into our preparations, but they don't need to know the details. "Don't let them see you sweat!" And besides, they go to a lot of effort when you're their guest.

17

"Hospicasualties"

Everyone has had at least one unforgettable hospitality moment that left them in stitches. One Sunday after church Steve and I stopped and asked a couple if they would like to come to our house for Sunday lunch. I hadn't planned on company, but I'd prepared some soup the day before. I knew I could throw something together. They agreed and followed us home.

As quick as a flash I put the soup on to heat, pulled some crackers out of the pantry, and began slicing cheese. About halfway through the meal I noticed we were running low on cheese. As I stood I said, "Excuse me, I need to cut some cheese." Everything got deathly quiet. I suddenly realized this phrase could refer to a certain bodily function. I hurriedly explained, and we all laughed. Nothing breaks the ice of an awkward situation more than the medicine of laughter.

Here are more humorous…or horrifying…stories, depending on your point of view, from women who responded to my survey.

- Our two-year-old daughter broke a ceramic dog that was in a basket by the fireplace. The host had noted what a special thing it was and that her daughter had given the treasure to her. I nearly died when I heard it crack. The next morning we hurried home, four hours away, and bought another one in a local specialty shop and had it overnighted to our host. It was the best we could do in a bad situation.

- My host took me to my room, and while I was in the bathroom she unpacked all my belongings, placing them in the closet and drawers. While I'm sure she meant well, I felt totally violated.

- My host had placed some bubble bath items near the tub, so I slipped into the soothing water and found a little "blow up" thing. I wasn't sure what it was, but I surmised it was a pad to sit on, so I did. It popped. I felt terrible! My hostess told me it was a neck pillow, and we both had a good laugh.

- My husband was taking a shower when the host came into the bathroom. When my guy called out, "Excuse me, I'm in the shower," she called back, "Don't worry, if you've seen one, you've seen them all." We couldn't wait to get out of there.

- I used the toilet and the worse thing that can happen, happened. I began to panic as the bowl began to overflow. Is there anything more horrifying than the helpless feeling of watching the toilet get closer and closer to the top and then, oops, there it goes down on the floor and out the door? I tried everything, but eventually I had to go tell my host.

- My husband decided that he was going to deep-fry the turkey for our first ever hosting of Thanksgiving dinner for our extended family. When it was finally done (which took two hours longer than we had planned) he dropped it on the sidewalk on the way into the house. Have you ever had all the fixings and none of the turkey?

- I tripped coming in the door, stumbled into the entryway, knocked over a vase that belonged to the host's mother and broke it. I announced, "Just call me Grace!"

- I planned for 40 and 70 showed up.

- I made and served a pecan pie for my company. I'm not good at making pie crust from scratch, so I bought an already prepared crust. I failed to remove the plastic covering on the bottom of the crust. Everyone kept saying that this was the "chewiest pecan pie they had ever eaten." Halfway through dessert one of my guests lifted his pecan filling up with his fork and up came a long piece of plastic.

- My husband began eating the centerpiece before the meal was served. It was a beautiful arrangement of colored grapes, but it wasn't a part of the dinner. I was terribly embarrassed, and I think the host was too.

- We were at a friend's new house for Thanksgiving dinner. The turkey grease started smoking. The smoke alarm went off and the couple didn't realize the alarm was connected to the fire station. We were shocked when the fire truck showed up.

- My host went to bed without telling me where I was supposed to sleep.

- My family and I arrived for a much anticipated visit—on the wrong day.

- When I blew out the candles on a birthday cake I got wax all over my host's beautiful tablecloth.

- My husband and I were invited to a dinner party. We accidentally sat at the head table and were asked to move.

- I ran up the stairs to hug my girlfriend, who was standing just inside the doorway. With my arms wide I ran straight into the unopened glass door.

- I cooked a lovely spaghetti dinner for my company. I made the sauce, salad, and garlic bread. I asked everyone to sit down to eat and then realized I hadn't cooked the pasta.

- My mother-in-law walked in on me when I was using the bathroom. I'm not sure who was more embarrassed.

- I didn't realize until my guests were seated and I was putting dinner on the table that the turkey wasn't precooked.

- I was suffering through menopause. My internal thermostat

was broken, and I was burning up inside. As soon as I got home, I tore my clothes off. When guests appeared at my door I had to yell for them to not come in. I gathered up my clothes and dashed for the bathroom. (I always wondered why my mom sat around with her top off until I went through menopause. Now I have such pity for her!)

Do any of these stories sound familiar to you? Or do you have some good ones of your own? If not, keep hosting and you will!

18

Inspiring Hospitality

D id you know showing hospitality can save your life? That's what happened to at least two families mentioned in the Bible!

A Very Wise Wife

When King David was being hunted by Saul, David and his men hid in the wilderness. They were in desperate need of supplies when David learned that Nabal, a local businessman, and his men were shearing sheep in the area. These were the same men David and his men had protected while they were doing their jobs. So David sent some young men to ask for food. Nabal, whose name means "fool," failed to show hospitality. He also insulted King David by saying, "Who is this David?" Nabal refused to give anything to David's men.

When word got back to David that his request for provisions had been rudely dismissed, he decided to teach the old sourpuss a lesson. He took 400 armed men with him to wipe out the Nabal household. When word of her husband's refusal got back to the lady of the manor, Mrs. Abigail, she went into full hospitality mode.

Abigail took 200 loaves of bread, 2 jugs of wine, 5 sheep already prepared, 5 measures of roasted grain, a hundred clusters of raisins, and 200 cakes of figs. She loaded them onto donkeys. Then she headed toward David, hoping to avoid the annihilation of her family.

The next time you're faced with an opportunity to
entertain guests, keep in mind that you may be saving
a life, finding a mate, or entertaining angels.

After appealing to the mercy of David, she took the responsibility for the lack of hospitality on herself. David accepted her gift and expressed his appreciation for her thoughtfulness. Ten days after the incident Nabal's heart became as stone and he died. And the lovely Abigail? David married her (1 Samuel 25).

An Intelligent Prostitute

The second family saved from extinction as a result of a woman who was willing to show hospitality was the family of Rahab. When two spies sent from Joshua came into the city of Jericho to spy out the land, they went to the house of Rahab, a harlot. She invited the men in and even hid them, risking her life and well-being. In defiance to her own people and king, Rahab protected the two men from discovery and gave them directions on how to avoid being caught once they left the safety of her home. As a reward for saving them, the men promised protection to Rahab and her family. She also eventually married one of the spies! Who would have thought being hospitable would be a great way to attract a husband?

The next time you're faced with an opportunity to entertain guests, keep in mind that you may be saving a life, finding a mate, or entertaining angels.

Hospitality—A New Testament Requirement

In early church times women who were widows and had no financial means (a husband, son, father, or father-in-law) were to be cared for by the church. Timothy offered some specific guidelines for women qualified to receive aid (see 1 Timothy 5:9-10).

Widows under the age of 60 were considered of "marrying age," and they were encouraged to do that. Those who were older than 60 were more likely to remain unmarried. These are the specific qualifications for a widow to be put on the list for church support:

- She was the wife of one man. This didn't exclude those women who had been married more than once. The phrase indicates she was with one husband at a time.

- She brought up children. This doesn't necessarily mean she had to give birth to a child. The meaning is more along the lines of having "nourished children."

- She washed the feet of the saints. This was a menial job often relegated to slaves. Since the unpaved roads were dusty or muddy, guests entering a house had their feet washed. It wasn't the act of washing someone's feet that qualified the widow as worthy of the church's care, but rather her spirit of humility and willingness toward service.

- She assisted those in distress—emotional, physical, mental, or even financial. She had proven by her past deeds that she could look beyond her own needs and see the hardship of others.

- She devoted herself to good work. The verb used in this phrase indicates an energetic, diligent pursuit of doing good deeds. She was willing to do whatever work needed to be done. Whether she spent her time taking care of her own household or reached out by helping the sick, visiting the imprisoned, or teaching and encouraging the younger women, she looked for opportunities to make a difference.

- She showed hospitality to strangers. Her home was open to foreigners, as well as friends and family. There were no hotels or motels in the ancient world and inns were often filthy and dangerous. Christians away from home depended on the hospitality of others. She was quick to provide shelter and food for those who came to her door.[1]

Biblical Hospitality Revealed

Throughout God's Word we're taught to extend hospitality. The following scriptures illustrate the need and the command to open our hearts, our doors, and our resources to others.

Genesis 18:2-8

When he lifted up his eyes and looked, behold, three men were standing opposite him; and when he saw them, he ran from the tent door to meet them and bowed himself to the earth, and said, "My Lord, if now I have found favor in Your sight, please do not pass Your servant by. Please let a little water be brought and wash your feet, and rest yourselves under the tree; and I will bring a piece of bread, that you may refresh yourselves; after that you may go on, since you have visited your servant." And they said, "So do, as you have said."

So Abraham hurried into the tent to Sarah, and said, "Quickly, prepare three measures of fine flour, knead it and make bread cakes." Abraham also ran to the herd, and took a tender and choice calf and gave it to the servant, and he hurried to prepare it. He took curds and milk and the calf which he had prepared, and placed it before them.

Genesis 24:17-20

Then the servant ran to meet her, and said, "Please let me drink a little water from your jar." She said, "Drink, my lord"; and she quickly lowered her jar to her hand, and gave him a drink. Now when she had finished giving him a drink, she said, "I will draw also for your camels until they have finished drinking." So she quickly emptied her jar into the trough, and ran back to the well to draw, and she drew for all his camels.

1 Samuel 25:18-19

Abigail hurried and took two hundred loaves of bread and two jugs of wine and five sheep already prepared and five measures of roasted grain and a hundred clusters of raisins and two hundred cakes of figs, and loaded them on donkeys. She said to her young men, "Go on before me; behold, I am coming after you."

1 Kings 17:9-11

"Arise, go to Zaraphath, which belongs to Sidon, and stay there; behold, I have commanded a widow there to provide for you." So he arose and went to Zarephath, and when he came to the gate of the city, behold, a widow was there gathering sticks; and he called to her and said, "Please get me a little water in a jar, that I may drink." As she was going to get it, he called to her and said, "Please get me a piece of bread in your hand."

2 Kings 4:8-11

There came a day when Elisha passed over to Shunem, where there was a prominent woman, and she persuaded him to eat food. And so it was, as often as he passed by, he turned in there to eat food. She said to her husband, "Behold now, I perceive that this is a holy man of God passing by us continually. Please, let us make a little walled upper chamber and let us set a bed for him there, and a table and a chair and a lampstand; and it shall be, when he comes to us, that he can turn in there." One day he came there and turned in to the upper chamber and rested.

Proverbs 3:28

Do not say to your neighbor, "Go, and come back and tomorrow I will give it," when you have it with you.

Matthew 10:40-42

He who receives you receives Me, and he who receives Me receives Him who sent Me. He who receives a prophet in the name of a prophet shall receive a prophet's reward; and he who receives a righteous man in the name of a righteous man shall receive a righteous man's reward. And whoever in the name of a disciple gives to one of these little ones even a cup of cold water to drink, truly I say to you, he shall not lose his reward.

Matthew 25:35-40

"For I was hungry, and you gave Me something to eat; I was thirsty, and you gave Me something to drink; I was a stranger, and you invited Me in; naked, and you clothed Me; I was sick, and you visited Me; I was in prison, and you came to Me."

Then the righteous will answer Him, "Lord, when did we see you hungry, and feed You, or thirsty, and give You something to drink? And when did we see You a stranger, and invite you in, or naked, and clothe You? When did we see You sick, or in prison, and come to You?"

The King will answer and say to them, "Truly I say to you, to the extent that you did it to one of these brothers of Mine, even the least of them, you did it to Me."

Luke 7:44-47

Turning toward the woman, He said to Simon, "Do you see this woman? I entered your house; you gave Me no water for My feet, but she has wet My feet with her tears and wiped them with her hair. You gave Me no kiss; but she, since the time I came in, has not ceased to kiss My feet. You did not anoint My head with oil, but she anointed My feet with perfume. For this reason I say to you, her sins, which are many, have been forgiven, for she loved much."

Luke 10:25-29,37

A lawyer stood up and put Him to the test, saying "Teacher, what shall I do to inherit eternal life?"

And He said to him, "What is written in the Law? How does it read to you?"

And he answered, "You shall love the Lord your God with all your heart, and with all your soul, and with all your strength, and with all your mind; and your neighbor as yourself."

And He said to him, "You have answered correctly; do this and you will live."

But wishing to justify himself, he said to Jesus, "And who is my neighbor?"…And he [the lawyer] said, "The one who showed mercy toward him."

Then Jesus said to him, "Go and do the same."

Luke 10:38-42

He entered a village; and a woman named Martha welcomed Him into her home. She had a sister called Mary, who was seated at the Lord's feet, listening to His word. But Martha was distracted with all her preparations; and she came up to Him and said, "Lord, do You not care that my sister has left me to do all the serving alone? Then tell her to help me." But the Lord answered and said to her, "Martha, Martha, you are worried and bothered about so many things; but only one thing is necessary, for Mary has chosen the good part, which shall not be taken away from her."

Luke 14:12-15

When you give a luncheon or a dinner, do not invite your friends or your brothers or your relatives or rich neighbors, otherwise they may also invite you in return and that will be your repayment. But when you give a reception, invite the poor, the crippled, the lame, the blind, and you will be blessed, since they do not have the means to repay you; for you will be repaid at the resurrection of the righteous.

Acts 16:15

When [Lydia] and her household had been baptized, she urged us, saying, "If you have judged me to be faithful to the Lord, come into my house and stay."

Romans 12:9-16,20-21

Let love be without hypocrisy. Abhor what is evil; cling to what is good. Be devoted to one another in brotherly love; give preference to one another in honor; not lagging behind in diligence, fervent in spirit, serving the Lord; rejoicing in hope, persevering in tribulation, devoted to prayer, contributing to the needs of the saints, practicing hospitality. Bless those who persecute you; bless and do not curse. Rejoice with those who rejoice, and weep with those who weep. Be of the same mind toward one another; do not be haughty in mind, but associate with the lowly. Do not be wise in your own estimation— but if your enemy is hungry, feed him, and if he is thirsty, give him a drink; for in so doing you will heap burning coals on his head. Do not be overcome by evil, but overcome evil with good.

2 Corinthians 9:6-9

He who sows sparingly will also reap sparingly; and he who sows bountifully will also reap bountifully. Each one must do just as he has purposed in his heart, not grudgingly or under compulsion, for God loves a cheerful giver. And God is able to make all grace abound to you, so that always having all sufficiency in everything, you may have an abundance for every good deed; as it is written "He scattered abroad, He gave to the poor, His righteousness endures forever."

Galatians 6:9-10

Let us not lose heart in doing good, for in due time we will reap if we do not grow weary. So then, while we have opportunity, let us do good to all people, and especially to those who are of the household of the faith.

Colossians 3:23

Whatever you do, do your work heartily, as for the Lord rather than for men.

1 Timothy 3:2-3

An overseer, then, must be above reproach, the husband of one wife, temperate, prudent, respectable, hospitable, able to teach, not addicted to wine or pugnacious, but gentle, peaceable, free from the love of money.

1 Timothy 5:9-10

A widow is to be put on the list only if she is not less than sixty years old, having been the wife of one man, having a reputation for good works; and if she has brought up children, if she has shown hospitality to strangers, if she has washed the saints' feet, if she has assisted those in distress, and if she has devoted herself to every good work.

Titus 1:7-8

For the overseer must be above reproach as God's steward, not self-willed, not quick-tempered, not addicted to wine, not pugnacious, not fond of sordid gain, but hospitable, loving what is good, sensible, just, devout, self-controlled, holding fast the faithful word which is in accordance with the teaching, so that he will be able both to exhort in sound doctrine and to refute those who contradict.

Hebrews 13:2

Do not neglect to show hospitality to strangers, for by this some have entertained angels without knowing it. Remember the prisoners, as though in prison with them, and those who are ill-treated, since you yourselves also are in the body.

James 1:27

Pure and undefiled religion in the sight of our God and Father is this: to visit orphans and widows in their distress, and to keep oneself unstained by the world.

1 Peter 4:7-11

Be of sound judgment and sober spirit for the purpose of prayer. Above all, keep fervent in your love for one another, because love covers a multitude of sins. Be hospitable to one another without complaint. As each one has received a special gift, employ it in serving one another, as good stewards of the manifold grace of God. Whoever speaks, is to do so as one who is speaking the utterances of God; whoever serves is to do so as one who is serving by the strength which God supplies; so that in all things God may be glorified through Jesus Christ.

1 John 3:16-18

We know love by this, that He laid down His life for us; and we ought to lay down our lives for the brethren. But whoever has the world's goods, and sees his brother in need and closes his heart against him, how does the love of God abide in him? Little children, let us not love with word or with tongue, but in deed and truth.

2 John 1:10-11

If anyone comes to you and does not bring this teaching, do not receive him into your house, and do not give him a greeting; for the one who gives him a greeting participates in his evil deeds.

Revelation 22:17

The Spirit and the bride say, "Come." And let the one who hears say, "Come." And let the one who is thirsty come; let the one who wishes take the water of life without cost.

The Greatest Invitation

All of us have received invitations of some type in our lifetimes. I've had my share of invites to dinner parties, birthday parties, anniversary celebrations, weddings, and business gatherings. I've been grateful for them all. Many of these I've attended, but some I politely turned down for various reasons. Of all the invitations that have been extended to me, my most treasured is the one given in the fall of 1969. It didn't come on paper, in an envelope, or via a phone call. It came straight to my heart. This song lyric by Steve best describes the greatest invitation, and I am eternally glad I accepted! I'm extending that invitation to you.

THE INVITATION

He met me at the door
Of the world where I'd been hiding
He said, "Come on in"
His eyes were so inviting
He looked past my outside
And straight into my heart
And when I went inside
I stepped out of the dark

Into the light
Lost to found
Death to life
No longer bound

By the chains
That held me to my sin
I bless the day
He invited me in

An invitation so rich with mercy
To a soul so sad and poor
O what joy I found when I went walking
Through Christ, the open door

Into the light
Lost to found
Death to life
No longer bound
By the chains
That held me to my sin
I bless the day
He invited me in[1]

Please RSVP

Anyone knows that when an important invitation is extended and accepted, what is worn to the event is very important. The call I received to become part of God's family exceeded all other invitations. Unfortunately all I had to wear into the presence of my Father in heaven were filthy rags. Isaiah 64:6 says, "For all of us have become like one who is unclean, and all our righteous deeds are like a filthy garment." But our loving Lord had that detail covered. He was gracious enough to provide the acceptable attire: "He has clothed me with garments of salvation, He has wrapped me with a robe of righteousness" (Isaiah 61:10).

ROBE OF RIGHTEOUSNESS

When I, a sinner, to you came
You saw the pity of my frame
In tattered rags of sin and shame
Unholy I came dressed

But like the Father clothed His wayward one
Who humbly from his sin returned
You clothed me with your holy Son
Now He's my robe of righteousness

He's my robe of righteousness
Over the body of this death
Not my own, but His alone
He's my robe of righteousness

Forever I will grateful be
That when Your eyes now fall on me
Your holy Son is who'll you'll see
He's my robe of righteousness[2]

Heidi and I pray and hope you'll accept this life-changing invitation.

Notes

Epigraph

1. Steve Chapman, "The Hands of Love," Times & Seasons Music, BMI, 2008. Used by permission.

Chapter 7—Showing Off or Showing You Care?

1. Martha was probably a widow and the oldest of three siblings. Martha's younger brother was Lazarus (John 11). Jesus is summoned to come to the aid of Martha and Mary when Lazarus dies. By the time He arrives, Lazarus has been dead for four days. Jesus then brings glory to God by raising him from the dead. Since her name is always mentioned first when naming the siblings, the general assumption is that she was the eldest.

2. Leland Ryken, James C. Wilhoit, Tremper Longman III, *Dictionary of Biblical Imagery* (Downers Grove, IL: InterVarsity Press, 1998), p. 402.

Chapter 9—Reaching In

1. Steve Chapman, "Everyone Within Me," Times and Seasons Music/BMI, 1992. Used by permission.

Chapter 10—Reaching Out

1. Steve Chapman, "Love Them Both," Times and Seasons Music/BMI, 1995. Used by permission.

2. Steve Chapman, "We Will Love This Child," Times and Seasons Music/BMI, 2005. Used by permission.

Chapter 11—Grandmas, Grandkids, and Hospitality

1. Heidi Chapman, "Home Is Somewhere," lyric, Times and Seasons Music/BMI, 2007. Used by permission.

2. Steve Chapman, "Lily Anne," Times and Seasons Music/BMI, 2005. Used by permission.

3. Steve Chapman, "When I Hear That Train," Times and Seasons Music/BMI, 2007. Used by permission.

Chapter 13—Santa Isn't the Only One Coming

1. Steve Chapman, "Mystery of the Season," Times and Seasons Music/BMI, 1992. Used by permission.

Chapter 18—Inspiring Hospitality

1. John MacArthur, *New Testament Commentary, 1 Timothy* (Chicago: Moody Press, 1995), p. 206.

The Greatest Invitation

1. Steve Chapman, "The Greatest Invitation," Times and Seasons Music/BMI, 2007). Used by permission.

2. Steve Chapman, "Robe of Righteousness," Times and Seasons Music/BMNI, 2007). Used by permission.

Recipe Index

To contact Annie Chapman or Heidi Chapman Beall,
or to find out more about Steve and Annie Chapman's speaking,
music, and books, or to get information on Heidi's ministries, write:

Steve and Annie Chapman
Heidi Chapman Beall
S&A Family, Inc.
PO Box 337
Pleasant View, TN 37146

or visit
www.steveandanniechapman.com

10 Things I Want My Husband to Know
Annie Chapman

You have been granted tremendous influence in the life of your husband. Whether he's the strong, silent type or an outgoing, gregarious guy, if he knows how much he means to you, he will excel in work and at home. But in the hustle of everyday life, it's easy to forget to let him know you...

- admire his work
- appreciate his thoughtfulness
- love how he interacts with the kids
- respect his opinion
- realize his need to spend time with hobbies or friends

From her 30 years as a wife, the wisdom of Scriptures, and the insights of husbands and wives, Annie provides practical suggestions for letting your husband know he is unequivocally loved. Whether you've been married 3 months or 20 years, your man will appreciate these words and actions, and you'll see amazing changes in your marriage.

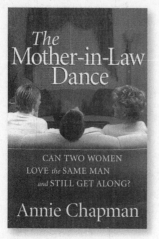

The Mother-in-Law Dance
Annie Chapman

Do you want to improve your relationship with your mother-in-law?

Could your relationship with your daughter-in-law be better?

Describing the often delicate relationship between mother-in-law and daughter-in-law as a dance, Annie candidly discusses the twists and turns of this connection and provides practical advice to help you better relate with your mother- or daughter-in-law. Drawing on years of experience, real-life input from other women, and biblical insights, she reveals simple steps to successfully—

- build a great relationship
- deal with new traditions and activities
- overcome hurts and conflicts
- set realistic boundaries
- handle generation-gap issues
- accept (and reject) advice
- cope with differences in faith

As you establish a rhythm of love and grace, you'll find that you and your in-law can become friends—even close friends. *The Mother-in-Law Dance* will help you make that journey to a respectful and loving relationship.